What People Are S

Pathway to th

Pathway to the Palace rings of truth for all of us and describes the importance of having a strong core. I had a trainer for a while who really helped me with exercise and spoke to me much about developing the core. *Pathway to the Palace* will help you develop a spiritual core, which is key. Without God as your core, situations can fall apart in your life. God bless you, Danette, for the strong word that you bring through this book.

—*Dr. Marilyn Hickey*
President, Marilyn Hickey Ministries

Pathway to the Palace is itself a standard setter! Danette's inspired writing addresses both the goals and pathways for developing Christian character. Her rich use of relevant biblical passages addresses practically every quality befitting of kingdom royalty, and her writing style makes the reading of challenging character issues light, inviting, and enjoyable. In essence, this book offers vision, hope, and promise for the high calling that God has placed on each and every Christian, regardless of the circumstances.

—*William F. Cox Jr., Ph.D.*
Professor and Director, Christian Education Programs,
Regent University School of Education

Pastor Danette writes with such passion that you can feel it pulsing in your soul as you read. Her genuine love for God shines forth from every page and creates a much-needed hunger within us to become standard setters. I was overjoyed to learn not just the scriptural guidance but also the practical, everyday things I could do to be an overcomer. This is a book for new believers and seasoned friends of God alike. Feel the unparalleled joy Pastor Danette exudes as you read her message.

—*Pastor Dan Willis*
Host, TCT Network television show *I'm Just Sayin'*
Senior Pastor, The Lighthouse Church, Chicago, Illinois

Pathway to the Palace contains a timely word for all generations. Each chapter inspires wisdom for all to live a life that rises above today's spiritual challenges and is for such a time as this.

—*Catherine Mullins*
International Song Writer & Worship Leader

Pathway to the Palace is written from the perspective of one who has lived and experienced the deeper dealings of God. Experience really is the best teacher, and Pastor Danette has opened her heart to you to share the many lessons life has brought her way. Only one who has walked this road understands the absolute necessity of obedience with integrity. It is a light on the path to being a standard setter!

—*Anne Gimenez*
Founder, the Rock Church, Virginia Beach, Virginia

Pathway to the Palace is a true delight. As a fellow minister with a special personal interest in the book of Esther, I was greatly rewarded by reading it. Pastor Crawford's practical applications of truth drawn from the biblical account of Queen Esther and many other biblical figures, as well as her own personal experiences, are right on target. The book spoke to and enriched me.

—*Richard Nicholson*
Regional Director, Assemblies of God World Missions

In a world infected with compromise leading to spiritual and moral decay, *Pathway to the Palace* offers a personal antidote to righteously provoke God's people to become something more. This book will knock you down, pick you up, and dust you off before launching you into that deeper, more fulfilling walk with God. *Pathway to the Palace* is not just a must-read; it's a study guide for a personal, life-changing experience with bountiful spiritual affects that will impact our circle of influence and ultimately determine our place in eternity with Jesus.

—*DJ Dozier*
Former running back, Minnesota Vikings and Detroit Lions
Former outfielder, New York Mets and San Diego Padres

There are women with the integrity and tenacity of Esther living today—modern-day standard setters—and Danette Crawford is one of them. This book isn't merely a theological discourse. It's the disclosure of Danette's journey to the palace of God's purposes in her own life. *Pathway to the Palace* is a navigational tool to help you make the right choices in order to reach God's kingdom destiny for your life and to assist others to do the same.

—*Pastor David S. Dillon*
Rock Church Franklin
Franklin, Virginia

When I first heard about *Pathway to the Palace* by Danette Crawford, my first thought was, "If this book is anything like her first book, *Don't Quit in the Pit*, it's destined to be another must-read." My assumption was correct. This is a book that warrants immediate attention in the kingdom of God.

—*Wade Trump III*
Pastor, Jamestown Christian Fellowship
Williamsburg, Virginia

Pathway
to the
PALACE

Becoming the Person of *Influence*
God Has Called You to Be

DANETTE JOY CRAWFORD

Pathway Publishing
Group

PATHWAY TO THE PALACE
Becoming the Person of Influence God Has Called You to Be

Danette Joy Crawford
P.O. Box 65036
Virginia Beach, VA 23467
www.joyministriesonline.org

ISBN: 978-0-578-09652-0
Copyright © 2012 by Danette Crawford
All Rights Reserved

Published by
Pathway Publishing Group
A media outreach of Danette Crawford Ministries
Virginia Beach, VA

1 2 3 4 5 6 7 8 9 10   21 20 19 18 17 16 15 14 13 12

DEDICATION

This book is dedicated to my daughter, Destiny. I love you so very much, and I know you are an Esther whom God has called for such a time as this! God is already using you mightily, but you haven't seen anything yet. The Lord has an anointing on your life to change the nation, and my prayer is that you will come into your full potential in God. You go, girl!

ACKNOWLEDGMENTS

First and foremost, I want to thank the Lord for His unfailing, unconditional love for me. Thank You, Lord, for saving my soul and allowing me the awesome privilege of ministering to Your people.

To my daughter, Destiny—thank you for filling my life with joy and laughter, and thank you for your patience and understanding during the many months that I have spent writing this book. I am so proud of you and your heart for God, and I know He is going to do great things through your life.

To my family and friends—thank you for believing in me and encouraging me along the way as I seek to fulfill God's calling on my life and as I walk in obedience to write every book the Lord has put in me.

To my spiritual mentors—thank you for being godly examples who have led the way for me to come into my full potential.

To the most awesome staff and intercessors anyone could ever have—the Joy Ministries Team. Thank you for standing with me through prayer, long hours of work, and your mountain-moving faith. Thank you for your passion for the Lord, your desire to see souls saved, and your heart to see lives changed. We truly are a team, and without you, Joy Ministries would not be what it is today.

To my most precious partners—without your generous gifts of time, prayer, and financial support, Joy Ministries could not do everything it is doing today. Thank you! Together, we are transforming lives, healing hearts, and winning souls.

A special thank-you to Greg and Jean, who remain my faithful partners and co-laborers in Christ. I love your heart to change lives, and you share in the fruit of every life changed through this book!

Finally, to my editor, graphic design team, and book agent—thank you for your heart to minister to people through the printed word. Thank you for believing in me and for being such a great team to collaborate with. It has been an honor to work with you all.

FOREWORD

The book of Esther tells a story that could have been written by an award-winning film writer in Hollywood: a queen is deposed, an orphan girl is elevated to a position of royalty, assassination plots are foiled, Jewish extermination is averted by a woman who would risk her life to stop it, and a villain who schemes to destroy his enemy is trapped and killed by his own instruments of destruction. The chronicle of this historical adventure is the foundation for the Jewish celebration of Purim, and this remarkable story has been inspiring and challenging readers, preachers, scholars, and authors for centuries. Now, it has become the framework of this profoundly insightful book by Danette Crawford, *Pathway to the Palace*.

I first met Danette Crawford when she appeared as a guest on *Praise the Lord*, a Christian talk show I frequently host. It was then that I discovered how genuine, sincere, and joyful she is. One quickly observes that she does all she can to welcome the Spirit of God. For years, Danette Crawford has demonstrated the divine calling on her life and ministry, through founding Joy Ministries Evangelistic Association, through hosting her television show, and through her travels as an evangelist. As if her plate isn't already full enough, she is a mother! A clear picture emerges of how dedicated, diligent, and dynamic this woman of God truly is. And now, God has continued to use her, this time as an inspiring author. We joyfully acknowledge her gift and the fact that the fingerprints of God are all over it.

Crawford writes that God is "calling all Esthers," but she emphasizes that this call extends to men and women, believers and nonbelievers. Her words spoke to my heart, and I was particularly struck by her down-to-earth style and personal approach. As you read, you will discover not only insights relative to Esther, Mordecai, and the host of other characters in the Bible story, but you will draw wisdom for your life from the experiences of Ruth, Joseph, and many others. This book is seasoned, steeped, and saturated with the Word of God, and Crawford speaks as a visionary, touching hearts and lives with every word. You will be challenged, as well, to live a godly life and examine your ways under the microscope of the living Word of God, thus preparing you for your place in the palace.

Pathway to the Palace provides insight, guidance, direction and encouragement and will be a welcomed addition to any Christian's library or bedside. So, sit back, relax, and allow the journey of reading this wonderful book to be your latest adventure in spiritual growth to the praise and glory of God.

—*Dr. Clifton Davis*
Internationally recognized minister and performer
Host of the Trinity Broadcasting Network show *Praise the Lord*

Contents

INTRODUCTION:
CALLING ALL ESTHERS

King Xerxes…commanded the seven eunuchs who served him…to bring before him Queen Vashti, wearing her royal crown, in order to display her beauty to the people and nobles, for she was lovely to look at. But when the attendants delivered the king's command, Queen Vashti refused to come. Then the king became furious and burned with anger. Since it was customary for the king to consult experts in matters of law and justice, he spoke with the wise men who understood the times and were closest to the king…. "According to law, what must be done to Queen Vashti?" he asked. "She has not obeyed the command of King Xerxes that the eunuchs have taken to her." Then Memucan [one of the nobles] *replied in the presence of the king and the nobles, "Queen Vashti has done wrong, not only against the king but also against all the nobles and the peoples of all the provinces of King Xerxes. For the queen's conduct will become known to all the women, and so they will despise their husbands and say, 'King Xerxes commanded Queen Vashti to be brought before him, but she would not come.' This very day the Persian and Median women of the nobility who have heard about the queen's conduct will respond to all the king's nobles in the same way. There will be no end of disrespect and discord. Therefore, if it pleases the king, let him issue a royal decree and let it be written in the laws of Persia and Media, which cannot be repealed, that Vashti is never again to enter the presence of King Xerxes. Also let the king give her royal position to someone else who is better than she. Then when the king's edict is proclaimed throughout all his vast realm, all the women will respect their husbands, from the least to the greatest."*

(Esther 1:10, 11, 15–20)

The rise of Esther from obscurity to royalty has inspired and challenged believers through the ages. It's hard to imagine having a chance to compete for the queen's crown! Harder still is imagining a queen, or any other celebrity figure today, being deposed on account of bad behavior. Queen Vashti was kicked out of the palace because she set a poor example for the kingdom. I wonder how many modern-day people in high positions would be able to retain them if they were held accountable for their actions as Vashti was!

Those who have a position of authority and influence, such as Vashti did, set a standard for society by their actions, attitudes, words—by every manner of self-expression. Looking at the culture around us, it's clear that those "role models" aren't setting a good example! Standards of morality, integrity, and ethics are at an all-time low in government, in the entertainment world, and even in the body of Christ. Character and standards go hand-in-hand because your standards are the product of your character; your character is what establishes your standards. And your character is who you really are when no one is watching. So, it follows that poor character creates low standards.

When Vashti set a standard of rebellion and disobedience, King Xerxes relieved her of her role so that the other women in his kingdom would not adopt her standard and defy their husbands. And then, he sent out a call for a new queen—one *"better"* than Vashti. The candidates for queen would have to undergo a series of tests to weed out anyone who did not qualify to be a standard setter.

> All of us have been called into ministry, whether or not we serve in a church or Christian organization that's labeled as a "ministry."

Our heavenly Father, the King of Kings, is looking for those who will be standard setters in His kingdom—shining examples for others to follow. What are your standards, and what do they communicate to those around you? The King of Kings and Lord of Lords is calling for a standard of excellence in character and in all areas of conduct. And, just as King Xerxes dismissed Vashti for her example of disobedience, the King of Kings will dismiss those who refuse to repent of their rebellious ways and fail to meet the standards of spiritual excellence He requires. The standard is nothing less than complete obedience. If the King does not demand a high standard, there will be no end to the disrespect and discord in His kingdom, as was feared in the day of King Xerxes.

Yes, God is a loving God, but He is also a just God who demands a standard of conduct that is appropriate for His subjects—His children, you and me. He demands such a standard because He loves us and wants what's best for us.

If you lower your standards and compromise your character, you could lose your position, just as Vashti did, and forfeit the privilege of having positive influence. Vashti was already in position. She had already been promoted to the palace. But her character couldn't keep her there. Her decision to flout the king's order and set a standard of disobedience cost her the throne.

The King is looking for standard setters. He is calling all Esthers. The call for Esthers is not just a call for women to arise and take their place in the body of Christ. The call for Esthers transcends gender, race, age, and nationality. The King has need of individuals with the character of Queen Esther and a willingness to be standard setters who model Christlike character, servant hearts, and righteous behavior.

All of us have been called into ministry, whether or not we serve in a church or Christian organization that's labeled as a "ministry." God doesn't have a hiring freeze on—He never has, and He never will. He's just looking for qualified applicants. Esther qualified! Esther wasn't from a picture-perfect background. Esther wasn't raised in the perfect home by the ideal family. Esther wasn't even from the right side of town, so to speak. But when the king called, Esther answered. It wasn't Esther's position that made her great. It was her great character and her willingness to answer the call that caused her to be promoted to queen, a position of greatness second only to the king. Esther was a world changer whose life and choices saved an entire nation.

The King of Kings is calling all Esthers to arise, report to the palace, and take their place as standard setters in His kingdom. Will you answer the call?

PART ONE

HEAR THE CALL

— 1 —

ME, CALLED?

Esther wasn't born at the top. She was an ordinary girl. Okay, so she was *"lovely in form and features"* (Esther 2:7), but the Bible doesn't say she was a bombshell or anything. Yet God used her to do extraordinary things. First Corinthians 1:27 says that *"God hath chosen the foolish things of the world to confound the wise; and God hath chosen the weak things of the world to confound the things which are mighty"* (KJV). Why does He do that? God loves to use those who seem the least likely to succeed or win because, when they do, He gets all the glory. God always does big things with small resources. He fed the five thousand with two little fish and five loaves of bread. God didn't use the artillery of a large army to defeat the giant Goliath; He used a small stone from a slingshot of a little boy named David.

When God uses someone like Esther—when He uses ordinary people like you and me—it gets everyone's attention. They all stand back in awe and say, "Only God could have done that!" And so God gets the glory.

When I started preaching on television, everyone who'd known me growing up said, "That has to be God!" I was the kid who always hid behind her mother's skirt. Speaking in front of people threw me into meltdown mode. But God turned my timidity into boldness so that He would get the glory, just as He got the glory when he took Esther, a common Jewish girl, and made her the queen of Persia.

Of course, God wants us to improve, to conform more and more to the image of His Son, Jesus. But He doesn't promote people because they are particularly gifted. God promotes servants—faithful servants! And all promotion comes from the Lord, as we learn from the Psalms: *"Promotion cometh neither from the east, nor from the west, nor from the south. But God is the judge: he putteth down one, and setteth up another"* (Psalm 75:6–7 KJV).

> **If you have a heart, you have the capacity to qualify as a standard setter. God wants you on His team!**

Esther was one of God's great leaders, but she wasn't promoted to a position of leadership because of her education, her pedigree, her wealth, or any other traits by which most people are promoted nowadays. It was her heart that qualified her for promotion. All of God's great leaders have been qualified because of their hearts—hearts that carry them through good times and bad, successes and failures, small triumphs and big messes, and cause them to come out pure. The heart of a person God promotes is a heart that's free of offense and bitterness and filled with love, gratitude, and forgiveness. If you have a heart, you have the capacity to qualify as a standard setter. God wants you on His team!

God in You Makes You Extraordinary

Even if nobody else believes in you, God does, and His opinion is the only one that counts. Maybe no one thinks you will make it. Maybe you've been told all your life that you'll never amount to anything. Maybe the enemy has whispered doubt and discouragement into your ears. Don't listen to him! Instead, choose to believe the truth—God's Word, which has the final say on who you are and what you are capable of.

God's Word is our manual for life, and we find this assurance in Proverbs 16:3: *"Commit to the LORD whatever you do, and your plans will succeed."* If we commit our every endeavor to the Lord, we will follow His lead and achieve ultimate success. It's when we try to get Him to follow our lead that we get into trouble! Later on in Proverbs 16, it says, *"In his heart a man plans his course, but the LORD determines his steps"* (verse 9). It doesn't work when we tell the Lord the path we're taking and ask Him bless it.

When we submit to the Lord's leadership, He will guide us into all truth (see John 16:13) and chart a clear course for us (see Proverb 3:5–6). If we commit everything we do to the Lord, we are headed in the right direction as we seek to fulfill our purpose and live as standard setters.

Esther fulfilled the call of God on her life to save her people, even though she was just an orphan girl. You and I can fulfill the call of God on our lives, as well, as long as we're obedient to submit to the God-ordained process that prepares us to answer that call.

Just Be Yourself

God has a tailor-made call for each one of us. But we'll never find success if we get wrapped up in pursuing someone else's call. Think of the process of building a house. If the foundation that's laid is designed to support a home with one story, any attempts to construct, say, an apartment complex on the site will fail, because those plans don't coincide with the foundation. A foundation can't support a structure it wasn't intended for. Similarly, God lays a foundation in each of our lives that will support what He plans to build in us and through us. He spends a great deal of time and attention laying our "foundations" of character, personality, giftedness, and anointing. And then, once the foundation is sound, He can add a superstructure of experiences that coalesce into a beautiful building that will never crumble, because the construction followed His blueprint.

You will always be the most anointed and the most effective when you are just yourself. If you try to be someone else, if you try to do things the way others do things, you lose your anointing. Esther was just an ordinary girl. She never tried to be someone or something that she wasn't. She was very comfortable in her own skin.

> You will always be the most anointed and the most effective when you are just yourself.

Similarly, David was an ordinary shepherd boy who was called to greatness—the king's throne, in fact. But his trip to the top was far from smooth. His first pitfall on his path to the palace was none other than the mistake of trying to be someone he wasn't. He tried to fight the giant Goliath dressed in someone else's armor because it seemed like the right thing to do. It didn't take him long, however, to realize that he would not succeed unless he was confident in who he was underneath his armor. David couldn't afford to try to be what others wanted him to be. He fought the giant and won only when he was who God had created him to be.

After King Saul had given David approval to fight Goliath,

Saul dressed David in his own tunic. He put a coat of armor on him and a bronze helmet on his head. David fastened on his sword over the tunic and tried walking around, because he was not used to them. "I cannot go in these," he said to Saul, "because I am not used to them." So he took them off. Then he took his staff in his hand, chose five smooth stones from the stream, put them in the pouch of his shepherd's bag and, with his sling in his hand, approached the Philistine....Reaching into his bag and taking out a stone, he slung it and struck the Philistine on the forehead. The stone sank into his forehead, and he fell facedown on the ground. So David triumphed over the Philistine with a sling and a stone; without a sword in his hand he struck down the Philistine and killed him.

(1 Samuel 17:38–40, 49–50)

David triumphed. David won. He was successful when he stopped trying to be someone else. "Little" David would grow up to be the best king Israel ever had, and God used him greatly, all because he started as an ordinary boy who wasn't afraid to be himself.

God is looking for giant killers in these last days. You don't have to be the biggest; you don't have to be the best trained or educated; you don't have to be voted "most likely to succeed." You don't have to be anything other than willing and obedient to be a giant killer.

Esther, too, was a giant killer. She stood in the face of an enemy bent on annihilating her people, and she pleaded on their behalf, but she did it all with complete confidence in who God had made her to be. You don't have to be a woman to be an Esther; you need only be yourself, but with the same character of heart as Esther. And it starts with a solid foundation of faith.

Firm Foundations

Esther was successful in her God-given assignment because she had a firm foundation of faith in the Lord. You, too, will arrive at the palace and fulfill your destiny if you allow the Lord to establish a strong foundation in your life.

When we have a strong, solid foundation in the Lord, He can build a large superstructure upon it. *Foundation* is defined as "the basis or groundwork of anything." The Lord delights to lay solid foundations in our hearts and lives because, just like in construction, the foundation is the most important part of the building. A firm foundation is vital for the success and sustainability of all that the Lord wants to build in and through our lives.

Your bedrock foundation—the basis on which your entire life should be built so that God can use you in His kingdom—is your relationship with the Lord. Before any significant building can take place in your life, you must have a solid foundation in your relationship with the Lord. The success of your ministry, your marriage, your business, and every other part of your life is based upon the foundation of your personal relationship with the Lord.

Many people, once they have a relationship with God, try to build a ministry or begin another significant endeavor without cultivating that relationship. You may have a foundation in Christ, but that doesn't guarantee that it will always be rock-solid. A habit of daily praying, studying the Word, worshipping the Lord, and living a godly life continually reinforces our foundation.

> *Therefore everyone who hears these words of mine and puts them into practice is like a wise man who built his house on the rock. The rain came down, the streams rose, and the winds blew and beat against that house; yet it did not fall, because it had its foundation on the rock. But everyone who hears these words of mine and does not put them into practice is like a foolish man who built his house on sand. The rain came down, the streams rose, and the winds blew and beat against that house, and it fell with a great crash.* (Matthew 7:24–27)

It's crucial that we build our lives on the Rock—the Lord Jesus Christ! Let's explore in greater detail the elements of a firm foundation, which is essential for every standard setter in God's kingdom.

The Word of God/Knowledge of Who You Are in Christ

An important part of every strong foundation is the Word of God, which is the authority on who you are in Christ. When I started in ministry, the first thing I needed to learn was my true identity in Christ. I was insecure and plagued with feelings of inferiority and rejection to the point where I could not function in my call. The turning point was graduate school. While I was working toward a master's degree in counseling, getting ready to minister emotional healing to others, the Lord did a tremendous work of healing in my life.

It was during those years that I really learned who I was in Christ. I was in a situation that forced me to face all of my hurts, my wounds, and my brokenness. After all, you can't minister emotional healing to others if you yourself are a broken mess! The Lord delivered me from many different roots of brokenness, several of which stemmed from the perceived lack of a father's love in my growing-up years. As I worked through the scars of my past by discovering and accepting my identity in Christ, I was ultimately able to embrace the bright future God had for me.

When you know who you are in Christ, you aren't controlled by what other people think about you. And I think we all know how powerful the opinions of others can be! Jesus Himself knew the sting of being doubted by others, for *"even his [Jesus'] own brothers did not believe in him"* (John 7:5). Don't expect that your situation will be any different!

Again, when no one else believes in you, remember that the Lord does. My biggest problem when I started graduate school was that I didn't believe in myself. I didn't believe that God could use me. I didn't see myself the way God saw me. But, as I submitted to the process of healing and restoration, I learned who I was in Christ. Finally, I could say with the psalmist,

> *For you created my inmost being; you knit me together in my mother's womb. I praise you because I am fearfully and wonderfully made; your works are wonderful, I know that full well. My frame was not hidden from you when I was made in the secret place. When I was woven together in the depths of the earth, your eyes saw my unformed body. All the days ordained for me were written in your book before one of them came to be.* (Psalm 139:13–16)

As I meditated on God's Word and its truths about who I was, I began to see myself as the Lord saw me. It didn't happen overnight; it was a process. But if we commit to going through the process, God will complete His great work in us and through us. The Word says that we can be confident of this very thing. (See Philippians 1:6.)

Praise

Another key element that reinforces your foundation is praise.

When the builders laid the foundation of the temple of the LORD, the priests in their vestments and with trumpets, and the Levites with cymbals, took their places to praise the LORD, as prescribed by David king of Israel.   (Ezra 3:10)

When you lead a life of praise, you have a grateful, thankful heart. If you are always talking about how bad things are, if you are always complaining about what you don't have, you will develop a heart that is bitter and ungrateful. Whatever you focus on becomes what you clearly see. If you aren't clearly seeing all of the blessings in your life, you aren't praising God as you should be.

> Whatever you focus on becomes what you clearly see. If you aren't clearly seeing all of the blessings in your life, you aren't praising God as you should be.

When my daughter, Destiny, was just two weeks old, my husband left me to raise her by myself. I was forced to live by faith at a higher level than ever before. I quickly learned a secret: If I focused on what I didn't have and wallowed in self-pity, I would get discouraged, overwhelmed, and even depressed. But if I praised God instead, thanking Him for everything I *did* have, I would begin to feel better as encouragement caused my faith to rise up in me.

So, I would walk around the house and pray out loud, saying, "Lord, I thank You that I have toilet paper. Lord, I thank You that I have soap in my shower. Lord, I thank You that You supply all my needs, according to Your riches in glory." (See Philippians 4:19.)

Believe me, I would thank God for every roll of toilet paper, because there were days when I didn't have any! We often lived on corn dogs and tuna fish for months at a time. But if I praised God in the midst of my storms, I maintained a thankful heart and kept my spirits up. Without a thankful heart of praise, it's very easy to get depressed. Without a thankful heart, it's very hard to see the blessings that you do have. But as we worship the Lord and praise Him daily for all of our blessings, faith and joy rise up within us. Make sure to count all your blessings instead of numbering your needs.

Purity and Righteousness

To be standard setters, we need to keep our foundations free from impurities—sinful thoughts, words, and actions. Picture a construction site where the foundation is being laid. When it's time to pour the cement, the area is blocked off to keep passersby from treading through the wet cement, tampering with the steel rods or rebar, and thereby spoiling the foundation. It's protected so that nothing will interfere with its structural integrity.

God does the same with our foundations. He wants to make sure they consist only in godly character. He doesn't want anything ungodly, such as deception and unforgiveness, to tamper with our foundation and compromise our structural integrity. Even the tiniest of "little white lies" compromises the strength of our foundation and opens the door to self-deception, which occurs when we try to justify our sins.

At Joy Ministries, the all-time record for the number of phone calls we have ever received for a single TV program was from a show I did called "The Deadly Deception of Unforgiveness." We must not have unforgiveness in our foundation. If we aren't careful, we can be deceived into thinking we have the "right" to hold on to unforgiveness. The Word speaks very clearly about this topic. For example, in Matthew 6:14–15, Jesus said, *"If you forgive men when they sin against you, your heavenly Father will also forgive you. But if you do not forgive men their sins, your Father will not forgive your sins."*

Wow—that's strong, but that's the truth! If we don't forgive others, our heavenly Father will not forgive us. People who harbor unforgiveness in their hearts live on shaky foundations, for a foundation can be solid only when it's full of mercy, not weakened by bitterness and resentment. Forgiveness is a choice, and as we choose to forgive others for even the most painful sins they've committed against us, we will be free and energized to give our best to God, producing great fruit in His kingdom.

Compromise is yet another impurity that weakens our foundation. Often, compromise is the result of listening to the enemy, Satan, who always tries to tear down whatever God is building. His desire is to steal, kill, and destroy whatever the Lord is building in our lives. (See John 10:10.) Remember, God has all power and authority. The devil doesn't have any authority in your life unless you open the door to him through compromise and sin. Beware of his tactics! Don't think that you can sin "a little bit" and get away with it, because the devil plays for keeps. Don't be tempted to "experiment" with illicit drugs, premarital sex, pornography, or anything else just because you plan to repent. The devil is trying to sneak in the back door and take you out. Don't allow it!

Faith and Hope

You also must not allow the devil or anyone else to cause you to doubt what God is building in your life. Discouragement is a nasty trick of the enemy, because if he can get you discouraged, he can get you to give up. That's his goal—to get you to quit in your "pit." He wants you to feel hopeless. If he can convince you that your situation is hopeless, the rest of his job will be easy; you'll quit on your own.

The truth is that you serve the God of hope. Remember Romans 15:13: *"May the God of hope fill you with all joy and peace as you trust in him, so that you may overflow with hope by the power of the Holy Spirit."* God is hope! And you can trust in Him, even in the deepest "pits" of life.

Hold on to hope and remember that God's plan for your life may involve developing your character in the pits of life. Once you get out of the pit and rise to the peak, He will use you to bring hope to countless other people!

Be Patient through the Building Process

A few years ago, a construction team broke ground on a lot near my office. Every time I drove past the site, I wondered what they were building, since they had not put up any signs that said "Coming Soon: _____." I got my hopes up that it would be my favorite restaurant or at least someplace fun. Yet, week after week, month after month, there was no indication as to what the finished product would be.

After a while, I grew pretty impatient. After all, months had passed, and nothing had been done beyond the foundation being laid. Finally, one day, when I returned from an out-of-town trip, I noticed that some progress had been made. But there still wasn't any sign telling me what to expect!

The next time I drove by the site, the framing was up, and the drywall was being hung. From that point on, drastic changes had been made just about every time I drove past. It was surprising how much progress they made in such small amounts of time. Finally, a sign appeared, and my curiosity was quenched: the building would be a set of storage units. Shortly thereafter, the project was completed, and the place opened for business.

Have you ever just wanted a sign? Something to clue you in as to what in the world God is trying to build in your life? Sometimes, we go through a long season of construction without any idea as to what the end result will be. And it's even harder to discern what's going on when a construction site is messy, and most of them are, with dust flying, jackhammers clamoring, and stuff strewn everywhere.

I have endured seasons of construction in which everything was messy for a while. Stuff was flying in every direction, and there was no sign in sight to tell me what the Lord was doing. It was only later on, once the foundation had been laid and the framing had begun, that I finally got a glimpse at what the Lord was building in my life.

> God is building something great *in* your life so that He can build something even greater *through* your life.

Maybe you have yet to understand the blueprint for God's building process in your life. Maybe you aren't aware of His timetable. If so, take courage—God is building something great *in* your life so that He can build something even greater *through* your life.

God doesn't want us doing average things for Him; He wants us doing great things. For that reason, He doesn't spend a moderate amount of time laying the foundation in our lives. No, He spends a great deal of time—sometimes years or even decades—to lay a solid foundation. But, once the foundation has been laid, the construction is completed in record time.

As we think about the process by which God lays a firm foundation in our lives, the word to keep in mind is *process*. Don't rush God along during construction. Don't jump ahead of schedule and start building your ministry, family, business, or other venture before His appointed time, or a structural collapse is likely to occur. Instead, relax and let the Master Builder build the foundation at His own pace. After all, He's the One holding the blueprints! Believe me, you want to be built up according to His divine plan and in His perfect timing.

Many years ago, I was growing impatient with the rate at which my ministry was growing. The Lord said to me, "I'm laying the foundation for a great ministry." When He said that, I was shocked that I was still in the foundation stages. Sometimes, it will take the Lord twenty or thirty years to lay a foundation. Don't rush the Master Builder! Keep in mind that the greater the end structure will be, the longer it will take to lay a proper foundation to support it. You'll be a standard setter before you know it.

Chapter 1: Me, Called?

Points to Ponder

1. God loves to do big things with small resources so that He gets all the glory. Can you think of an example from your own life—or from the experience of someone you know— when God took a seemingly impossible situation and turned it around? How did this affect your faith in Him?

2. We saw that David triumphed over Goliath only when he was himself—when he took off King Saul's armor and stopped trying to be the king. Have you ever tried to be someone you weren't, only to have your plans backfire? How can an understanding of who you are in Christ help you to accept yourself for you?

3. Consider the role of praise in your relationship with God. How often do you praise Him? And through what type(s) of expressions of praise do you seem to draw closest to Him? Reflect on these questions and then try to think of ways to incorporate praise more fully into your foundation.

4. Have you ever been tempted to "park in the pit"? How did your faith in God help you to climb out? (If you're still in a pit, try to identify what got you there, then pray for discernment about finding a way out.)

Meditate on these Scriptures, speak them aloud, and commit them to memory:

Trust in the Lord *with all your heart and lean not on your own understanding; in all your ways acknowledge him, and he will make your paths straight.*   (Proverbs 3:5–6)

Commit to the Lord *whatever you do, and your plans will succeed.*
(Proverbs 16:3)

For you created my inmost being; you knit me together in my mother's womb. I praise you because I am fearfully and wonderfully made; your works are wonderful, I know that full well.   (Psalm 139:13–14)

My God will meet all your needs according to his glorious riches in Christ Jesus.   (Philippians 4:19)

— 2 —

FINE-TUNE YOUR FOCUS

Picture yourself at the palace, along with all of the other candidates for queen. I'm sure many of them were daydreaming about what it might be like to wear the crown and sit on the throne. But daydreaming didn't get them anywhere, because daydreaming is very different from having a dream. Daydreaming is entertaining a fruitless fantasy about a desired outcome; it puts no action or effort into making that outcome a reality. Daydreams come at a cheap price—just a few hours or moments of your time. But a dream costs you everything—time, effort, and, perhaps most of all, focus.

Esther was a woman of focus. Her focus not only took her all the way to the king's chambers; it kept her there permanently. Focus enabled Esther to win the heart of the king and to blow the competition out of the water.

When a woman is in labor, about to give birth, she is told to choose a "focal point" to help her breathe and tune out all distractions. You will never birth anything without focus! Plenty of people have dreams, but those dreams never come to fruition without focus. Focus gives birth to fruit. Many people are trying to be fruitful, but they aren't focused. When you try to be fruitful in your business, your ministry, or your family, but you lack focus, you will get discouraged and be tempted to throw in the towel. You will find yourself trying to do things in your own strength, which inevitably results in discouragement and burnout.

Desire or Passion?

If I were to ask you if you had a desire to be used by God to change lives, most of you would say yes, especially now that you know God wants to use you. Every time I have asked this question during a conference or in a service, the vast majority of people raise their hands. Most of you desire to use your gifts and talent for kingdom purposes.

But the Father wants us not only to have a desire to be used; He wants us to have a passion for His purpose. Desire is different from passion because passion involves a higher degree of focus. Desire will take us to a certain level, but passion will take us all the way to the palace.

> **Desire will take us to a certain level, but passion will take us all the way to the palace.**

When passion backs our commitment, nothing stops us. People with passion don't get burned out. People with passion don't find their identity and security in their work or their performance. People with passion press their way long after those with desire quit the race.

When you merely desire something, you are always assessing the price you'll have to pay in order to obtain it. When it's your desire, you even try to negotiate the price. You try to make a deal, and you might say, "Okay, I'll do this if I get paid this much." "I will do this as long as I can still do that."

When you possess passion, you are willing to forsake everything—personal comforts, carnal desires—and pay the price, no matter how high. Nothing stops you—not discouraging words, not self-doubt, not the demeaning attitudes of others. Passion is focused on paying the price, no matter how severe the inconvenience, no matter how high the cost, no matter how extreme the demands.

A *desire* is "a longing or craving, as for something that brings satisfaction or enjoyment." Does that ring a bell? Desire is all about me, me, me—what I want, what I crave. But passion is different. Passion is stronger than desire. And passion has a different focus. The dictionary defines *passion* as "any powerful or compelling emotion or feeling." When we have a passion to be used by God, it's all about His plan, not ours. When passion directs our focus toward the Lord and His purposes, rather than selfish desires and personal gain, nothing can stop us from finishing the race and fulfilling the call.

> *And now, compelled by the Spirit, I am going to Jerusalem, not knowing what will happen to me there. I only know that in every city the Holy Spirit warns me that prison and hardships are facing me. However, I consider my life worth nothing to me, if only I may finish the race and complete the task the Lord Jesus has given me....* (Acts 20:22–24)

Paul was compelled by the Holy Spirit—it was his passion. And because it was his passion, he didn't allow anything to stop him—not shipwrecks, not prison stints, not others' words or opinions, not snake bites, nothing!

The Fruit of Focus

God has called you to a royal position, but you'll need focus to get there. Focus is a ticket to your palace and a sure way not to buckle under the palace pressures once you get there. A lot of people want fruit without focus, but it never happens that way. Focus will cost you something. It will cost you your will and your way, just for starters! Many people lose their focus because things are not happening fast enough for them. Since they don't see instant results, they move on to something else, never allowing the Lord to bring them all the way to their palace, or their destiny in the Lord.

Once you catch a glimpse of the Lord's call on your life, don't lose sight of what the Lord is building or be tempted to give up because He's taking too long, in your opinion. I want to share a story with you that I heard a few years ago.

A man was passing by a construction site, and he stopped to ask one of the tradesmen what he was doing. The worker replied gruffly, "I'm laying bricks, can't you see that?" The man watched a while longer and then asked another worker the same question. "I'm just earning a living," he replied. The man asked the question of a third worker, who replied, "I'm building a cathedral."

There is no doubt in my mind that the quality of work by the third man, not to mention his sense of purpose and significance, was far superior to that of the first two. The third man had a vision—he saw the big picture, and he was focused on the finish line rather than the somewhat tedious task at hand. God wants to build your life into a beautiful cathedral. Focus on the finish so that you'll make it there!

There are many starters in life but few finishers. It's easy to get excited about a prophetic word over your life that says you will bless people all over the world. But the day-to-day focus that is required to see that call fulfilled is another story.

When you have a kind of focus that is appropriate for standard setters, it will manifest itself in the following facets, or fruits.

Focus Overcomes Distractions

Esther was a finisher because she focused on the finish line and didn't allow the setbacks of life to distract her. Winners never quit, and quitters never win. Winners are always focused on the finish line, the final product. You might be the most talented, the most gifted, or the most skilled, but if you aren't focused, you are likely to quit long before reaching the finish line.

If we aren't focused, we're apt to be derailed from the pursuit of our purpose by the tiniest of distractions. The enemy is always trying to steal our focus with distractions and detours that prevent us from fulfilling the will of the Father. And he succeeds only when we turn our focus inward and dwell on selfish needs, wants, and desires.

Distractions often come in the form of discouragement, accusations, oppression, or depression. To *distract* means "to draw away or divert, as the mind or attention; to disturb or trouble greatly in mind; beset." The enemy always wants to draw your attention away from God and to direct it toward himself. He wants to draw you away from what the Lord has called you to do, and he wants you to waste your time, your attention, and your energy on fruitless distractions.

If we are to resist the devil's distractions, we need to focus on the will of the Father and be passionate about carrying it out. We can't afford to focus on ourselves. When we are fueled by our passion and unwavering in our focus, we can shake off every distraction and pull through to the end, just like the apostle Paul.

The Holy Spirit compels us towards our purpose and our "palace." But it's up to us not to repel His compelling! *Repel* means "to thrust back or away; to resist effectively." Don't repel the Holy Spirit!

When the Holy Spirit compelled Paul to go into Jerusalem, Paul didn't reject His leading. Even though he had been through the wringer and probably expected more of the same in Jerusalem, he didn't squelch his passion or lose his focus. He knew where the Lord was leading him, and he focused on getting there, no matter the cost to him personally.

The Holy Spirit may compel us to do any number of things—give sacrificially to a ministry, participate in a local outreach or an overseas mission trip, call a friend, or go out of our way to encourage someone we don't even know. Don't ever repel the compelling of the Holy Spirit, for God has great fruit waiting for you at the finish line of your focus!

The apostle Paul wrote, *"Yet when I preach the gospel, I cannot boast, for I am compelled to preach. Woe to me if I do not preach the gospel"* (1 Corinthians 9:16). When Christ's kingdom is our passion, it compels us to live for Him, to draw others to Him, and to set a standard of excellence in His kingdom. It's not all about us; it's all about Him.

Second Corinthians 5:14–15 says, *"For Christ's love compels us because we are convinced that one died for all, and therefore all died. And he died for all, that those who live should no longer live for themselves but for him who died for them and was raised again."*

Our passion for the Lord compels us to focus on Christ and forgo personal comforts for the sake of the call. When we are focused on the Lord and passionate about His work, we will be able to echo Jesus and say, "Father God, not my will but Yours be done." (See Matthew 26:39; Mark 14:36; Luke 22:42.)

Esther's passion for her purpose—preserving God's people—kept her focused at the palace. And your passion for saving souls and exhorting others to live with righteous character will keep you focused as you step into your purpose in God.

Focus Fulfills the Mission

Once Esther arrived at the palace, she needed focus more than ever. After all, she didn't want to suffer the same fate as Vashti! When Esther got to the palace, she was surrounded by great riches, yet she didn't get caught up in what I call the "hoopla." She stayed focused on her purpose. She knew why God had put her in that position. She understood that God hadn't placed her in the palace for her own renown but for the sake of the people she would save from destruction.

If you lack focus, you can lose sight of why God put you in the palace, and you may end up falling short of the call because you're caught up in enjoying the hoopla. God wants to bring each of us to our palace for the sake of His people. If you aren't properly focused before you get to the palace, you will lose focus quickly once you get there.

Many people start out wanting to help hurting, broken people—that's what ministry is all about. But, somewhere along the line, they end up wanting to be famous. They lose their focus once they reach the palace. Jesus is the famous One, and, when you have proper focus, you never forget it.

Focus Finishes in Spite of Frustrations

Your circumstances may change overnight, for better or for worse, but you can't let them cause you to lose your focus. When I became a single mom of a newborn baby, it happened overnight. Yet I had to maintain my focus on fulfilling God's call on my life. Was it easy? No! Was it possible? Yes, but only when I relied on Christ for strength.

Esther is a great example of someone who maintained her focus in the face of life's challenges. We know that she was orphaned at an early age, a devastating experience that could have crippled her emotionally and spiritually, if she had allowed it to. She could have gotten mad at God and questioned Him, saying, "Why in the world did You allow my parents to die?"

Have you ever questioned God? I don't believe it's wrong to question God, but it is wrong to allow your questions to develop a gap between you and Him. We must understand that we don't have to understand everything—in fact, we never will! But when we trust in the Lord with all of our hearts, our lack of understanding ceases to matter. The Bible tells us to *"trust in the LORD with all your heart and lean not on your own understanding; in all your ways acknowledge him, and he will make your paths straight"* (Proverbs 3:5–6).

> God wants to bring each of us to our palace for the sake of His people.

We get into trouble when we try to lean on our own limited understanding. We can actually fall when we are attempting to lean on the wrong thing. Esther never fell; she stood strong. I'm sure it was painful. I'm sure she had a lot of questions. Yet she maintained her focus and never compromised her character. For these reasons, she landed in the palace.

When we go through difficult times, we can focus on all the difficult things we have been through. We can whine and complain about how bad we have it. Or, we can count our blessings in the midst of it all. For those of us who have been through some storms, we should be praising God that we didn't die there! If you are reading this book, you are alive. Thank God that He's brought you through every storm thus far! It may not have been easy, it may not have been pretty, but the truth is that you're alive, and so is Jesus. You are both alive and well. You and God are the majority, no matter the odds, so keep focusing forward.

After Job had endured unspeakable hardships, God blessed him with double for his trouble. And Job never looked back. Yes, it was a painful season. Yes, it was a bummer at the time. But, God got the glory and Job was restored to double of what he had before!

Don't focus on the trouble; focus on the double!

Don't focus on the trouble; focus on the double! Your reaction will determine your destiny. If you get angry and bitter, if you curse God and choose to die in your storm, then that's how your story will end. But, if you decide to get up out of your mess and go forward, the Lord will be right there, loving you all the way to the other side, if you'll simply focus on Him. He'll even carry you to the other side! There have been many storms that the Lord literally carried me through, and He will do the same for you.

If you are faced with challenging circumstances today, don't think you are the only one. One of the tricks of the enemy is to get you to think that you are the only one who has ever felt the way you are feeling. He tries to convince you that you are the only one who has ever been in your situation. He whispers in your ear, "No one loves you or cares about you, not even God." Don't buy the lie. Don't focus on yourself. Esther wasn't focused on herself and what she was going through. She was focused on her future and all that God had for her. Focus took Esther all the way to the palace, and it will do the same for you.

Focus Refuses to Quit

Psalm 34:19 says, *"Many are the afflictions of the righteous, but the L*ORD *delivers him out of them all."* Yes, we will go through difficult times, but the key word is *through*. Be determined not to camp there but to keep walking in obedience all the way through. I promise you will reach the other side. The Lord promises to bring us through, but we have to make the decision not to quit.

The twenty-first chapter of Acts gives us a run-down of the tough experiences the apostle Paul endured, which I briefly mentioned before. Next to Job, I think Paul was at the top of the list for enduring difficult times. While Paul was in Jerusalem, the crowd dragged him from the temple and beat him brutally, intending to kill him. The commander of the Roman troops arrested Paul and ordered him to be bound in chains.

Yet, as Paul was being hauled off to prison, he asked permission from the commander to speak to the crowd, and he started to share his testimony. Talk about not quitting! He wasn't distracted from his purpose. He continued to preach the gospel no matter what.

When we have the focus of Paul, we will be distraction-proof and can be determined never to quit. The reason the enemy wants to distract us, the reason the enemy wants us to feel hurt and rejected, is because he wants us to quit and give up.

Paul just kept on keeping on! After he was shipwrecked and finally got to shore, a viper came out of the fire and bit him. What did Paul do? He shook it off. He refused to let his problem stop him. Quitting wasn't an option.

If you will determine ahead of time to never quit, you, too, can complete your purpose in record time. Flirting with the idea of quitting is not wise. Quitting is not an option, so don't even entertain the thought. God has too many good things just waiting for you on the other side of this obstacle.

Chapter 2: Fine-Tune Your Focus

Points to Ponder

1. Summarize the distinction between a *desire* and a *passion*.

2. Now, compare and contrast the nature and outcomes of (a) a *desire* you've felt with (b) a *passion* you've adopted.

3. What are some of the most significant distractions that tend to detour you on your pursuit of a particular God-given passion? How can you work on eliminating them and focusing on the finish, instead? Consider finding an accountability partner to pray for you and to check to see how well you're overcoming these distractions.

4. Have you ever questioned God? If so, you aren't alone; many believers do that very thing when faced with a difficult situation or painful problem. Did He answer you? In what way?

5. Think about a time when you were sorely tempted to quit. Can you identify the tactics of the devil that were the most effective at wearing down your determination? Think about the apostle Paul and all he endured, and then memorize some Bible verses, such as those below, to recite when the devil is wearing you down.

Meditate on these Scriptures, speak them aloud, and commit them to memory:

Many are the afflictions of the righteous, but the LORD delivers him out of them all.   (Psalm 34:19)

Set your minds on things above, not on earthly things. (Colossians 3:2)

I press on toward the goal to win the prize for which God has called me heavenward in Christ Jesus.   (Philippians 3:14)

Whatever is true, whatever is noble, whatever is right, whatever is pure, whatever is lovely, whatever is admirable—if anything is excellent or praiseworthy—think about such things.   (Philippians 4:8)

— 3 —

TRUST IN GOD'S TIMING

One day, Esther was living an ordinary life, and the next day, she found herself in the palace. When God's will and God's timing intersect, suddenly, we are thrust into our purpose and place in God. The key is to wait for His appointed time to arrive.

Esther was hidden in obscurity until the Lord's appointed time. God alone knew all along what He had in store for her. No one, not even Esther herself, could have anticipated how He would work through her!

Timing is key. If Esther had not arrived at the palace at the time that the Lord had ordained, she would have missed her appointment with destiny. Prior to the king's decision to start the selection process for a new queen, there was no place for Esther at the palace. The position wasn't even open. King Xerxes was not yet ready for a new queen. And if Esther had dragged her feet instead of answering the call, she would have been too late; the position would have been filled already.

Standard setters are strategically positioned by the Lord to uphold His truth in a chosen season. Again, patience is key, because it doesn't work when we rush God along and try to declare a season before its time has come.

Favor for Each Season

Genesis 18:14 says, *"Is anything too hard or too wonderful for the Lord? At the appointed time, when the season [for her delivery] comes around, I will return to you and Sarah shall have borne a son"* (AMP).

God fulfilled His promise to Abraham and Sarah at His appointed time. We need only to wait for God's timing, for He has an appointed time for each season. Seasons come and go automatically. We can't prevent a season from coming when it's God's time—that season just comes! Just as we can't force winter to end and spring to begin, we can't rush the seasons of God's kingdom. We can only embrace every transition and trust that God's favor follows us into every new season.

If we don't wait patiently for a season, we get stressed out and discouraged for no reason. We end up wasting time and energy. If we try to hang on to an old season and try to delay the next one's arrival, problems emerge. There is nothing that we can do to prevent a new season from coming, nor can we slow it down—the schedule is in God's hands.

All we need to do is remain attuned to the passage of God's seasons so that we don't miss ours when it comes. Continue on your journey of spiritual maturation, and you will be ready for the approaching season. It will be here before you know it!

God's Timing Is Perfect

God is always right on time.

Don't tell me that God is not an on-time God. Oh yes, He is! He's never early, and He's never late. It can be tempting to set a deadline for God, but many people consider Him late, even if He shows up on that day, all because they saw no indications of His help prior to the deadline. Nobody knows this more than I do. I have been a single mom since my daughter was two weeks old, and my early years of parenting presented many challenges, including financial hardship. Every month, I would get so worried and stressed out, thinking I would be late with my mortgage payment. Well, it was never paid late—in fact, not one of my payments was tardy. God's provision for me was always right on time, but it would often arrive the day my bills were due. Waiting until the last minute freaked me out! I was a slow learner, but I did finally learn that God is always right on time.

God's provision for Ruth was right on time, too. There's no record of her panicking that she wouldn't find provision for herself and her mother-in-law. She simply kept going forward in her faithfulness. As we take one step of obedience at a time, faithfully following the direction of the Lord, provision will always be there in the season when we need it—right on time.

God's Great Leaders Understand God's Timing

When God's timing and God's will intersect, suddenly, the promises of God are fulfilled. Then and only then does God move at the speed of "suddenly." Leaders must realize this truth so that they may discern God's seasons and move within them according to His plan.

You may wait for thirty years for your suddenly. But when God's will and God's time intersect, it will be suddenly that the promises of God are fulfilled. This truth is evident in the lives of a number of key people in the Bible, including Jesus Himself.

Jesus

The Bible says, *"But **when the time had fully come**, God sent his Son, born of a woman, born under law, to redeem those under law, that we might receive the full rights of sons"* (Galatians 4:4–5, emphasis added).

"When time had fully come," Jesus was born. His birth wasn't a day early; it wasn't a day late. It occurred at God's divinely appointed time.

Years later, during the wedding at Cana, Jesus performed the first of His miracles but made sure His mother, Mary, knew that His greatest miracle was not ready to manifest. When the wine had run out, Mary hinted that Jesus ought to help, and He replied, *"Dear woman, why do you involve me?...My time has not yet come"* (John 2:4).

The hour for Jesus' death and resurrection, which would supply the world with an inexhaustible source of *"living water"* (see, for example, John 4:10–11), had not yet arrived. Other people may have been trying to push the season, but when it isn't God's time, it simply isn't time!

Joseph

*Joseph had a dream, and when he told it to his brothers, they hated him all the more. He said to them, "Listen to this dream I had: We were binding sheaves of grain out in the field **when suddenly** my sheaf rose and stood upright, while your sheaves gathered around mine and bowed down to it."*
(Genesis 37:5–7)

God had shown Joseph his "suddenly" from the very beginning, but it came only after God had built the necessary character in his life—a time-consuming process. Yet Joseph didn't disqualify himself by complaining or quitting in the face of slavery, imprisonment, or any other hardships that stood between him and his "suddenly." He persevered, passed the test, and made it to the palace in God's perfect timing.

Ruth

Ruth arrived with her mother-in-law, Naomi, in Bethlehem at just the right time, *"as the barley harvest was beginning"* (Ruth 1:22). Her timing could not have been better, because it was in the field in the middle of harvest time that Ruth met Boaz, the man who would become her kinsman-redeemer and husband. If she had arrived before or after the barley harvest, her path and Boaz's would not have crossed to create a divine opportunity.

Because of the timing of Ruth's arrival, *"she went out and began to glean in the fields behind the harvesters. As it turned out, she found herself working in a field belonging to Boaz, who was from the clan of Elimelech"* (Ruth 2:3). *"As it turned out"*—did you catch that phrase? It just so happened that Ruth arrived in Bethlehem with her mother-in-law as the barley harvest was beginning, and it just so happened that she gleaned in the fields of a man named Boaz. It wasn't a coincidence. It was God's divine appointment. The Lord was ordering Ruth's steps, and because she was obedient to follow the Lord's leading and timing, she stepped into her destiny.

God knew the big picture. He was strategically setting Ruth up to meet Boaz, and He brought her to Bethlehem just in time to receive her "Boaz blessing."

Prepare for Sudden Promotions and Turnarounds

For Jesus, turnaround time was the resurrection. Everyone feared the worst when Jesus was crucified on the cross, but it wasn't over. Three days later, it was appointed that He should rise again. Your life isn't over, either! Turnaround time is coming for you. Father God is about to resurrect dead dreams, delayed visions, and dwindling hope.

After many years of faithfulness through hardships, Joseph was suddenly promoted. After losing it all, Job suddenly stepped into a double portion of blessings. Although both of these men endured challenging times, neither one grew impatient with God. Because they trusted His timing, they were rewarded with sudden promotion. And I believe the same will be true for you today. It's promotion time. Welcome to the season of suddenlies!

I believe God is working behind the scenes to set the stage for your "suddenly." If you aren't expecting your "suddenly," though, you won't be prepared when the time comes. In the season of "suddenlies," the dreams and visions you've been harboring for years suddenly come to pass. Suddenly, you are promoted. Suddenly, everything God has told you would happen begins to transpire. Suddenly!

Ruth's "suddenly" came as a result of her character, which earned her favor in the eyes of Boaz. She acknowledged her lowly position to him, saying, *"You have given me comfort and have spoken kindly to your servant—though I do not have the standing of one of your servant girls"* (Ruth 2:13). Although she did not have the position, her character and favor opened the door for her suddenly.

In the season of suddenlies, overnight people who had the position suddenly lose it due to their lack of character, while those who did not have the position but exhibit good character suddenly get it! When you are in the season of suddenlies, everything that you have done in secret gets rewarded outwardly. Suddenly, people begin to notice you. Suddenly, you find favor in the eyes of those in high places. One minute, you're gleaning in the field; the next minute, you own the field! This was true of Ruth, who suddenly stepped into the position of owner when she married Boaz.

When you find favor with the Lord in the season of suddenlies, everything that belongs to Him suddenly becomes yours. Suddenly, you go from the bottom to the top. Suddenly, the last are first, and the first have taken the backseat! (See Matthew 20:16.)

Just as favor ushered Esther and Joseph into their palace position in God, suddenly, the favor of God will usher you into your palace position. Don't give up during the difficult times. You will be promoted. The favor of God that was on Joseph and Esther is on you today. You are covered in God's love and His favor everywhere you go, no matter what the season!

Purposeful Positioning

God loves us so much that He strategically positions and then prepares us for our purpose. The positioning process often looks entirely different from our expectations. God positioned little David with a few little sheep on the backside of the desert, but God was preparing him for his purpose—to defeat a giant named Goliath!

Joseph was positioned for his purpose right there in the pit. Yes, the pit can be a place of great preparation, as long as you keep your heart right during your "pit stops." God picks the most effective place of preparation for each of us, and we need only submit to the positioning process.

> The pit can be a place of great preparation, as long as you keep your heart right during your "pit stops."

Once we are positioned for our purpose, we are prepared at that place of positioning. Joseph was positioned in the pit, but his preparation had only just begun. In the pit, he underwent preparations for the prison, where he underwent preparations for the palace.

There are no coincidences in God, only divine appointments. As we just do the right thing—what we are supposed to do—we will trip over the will of God and the blessings of God for our lives. Ruth just ran right into her Boaz blessing. She wasn't thinking about herself. She wasn't looking for her blessing. She was just working hard at doing the right thing or the "righteous" thing. As you and I do the same in our lives, we will "trip over" the will of God and all of His blessings.

Look Past Appearances, for God Alone Picks Our Place of Positioning

I would like to take a moment to caution you about misinterpreting what may look like the perfect place or the place God would have you to be.

Let's consider Ruth again. Because she was in the right place at the right time and with a right heart, she ran right into her "Boaz blessing": a man to love her, care for her, and provide for her. But notice this about Ruth: she wasn't thinking about herself or looking specifically for a blessing. Instead, she was just working hard at doing the right thing.

The "Boaz blessing" symbolizes a place of abundant provision, whether spiritual, emotional, or physical, that *results from obedience, commitment, and faithfulness.* So many women are waiting for a man to arrive on the scene as their "Boaz blessing," but they don't realize that this type of blessing is a place in God where the blessings of the Lord are released in abundance on those whose character and integrity resemble Ruth's. Furthermore, many women are quick to seize upon a person or situation that appears to be a blessing from God, only to find themselves trapped in a relationship of abuse and harm. This seems to be especially true of single women longing for a husband. They often rush God's timing and unite themselves with the first man who comes along, only to regret it later.

> Rest assured that God will connect you with the right channels once you have stepped into the proper season.

I can honestly say that I have crossed over into the "Boaz blessing" in my own life—and I'm as single as single can be! I'm a single mom with no prospects in sight. But I know that my provision comes not from man but from God.

I also recognize that the "Boaz blessing" is one form of the biblical principle of sowing and reaping: *"A man reaps what he sows"* (Galatians 6:7). Ruth sowed provision, faithfulness, and love into the life of her mother-in-law, Naomi, and she reaped what she had sown: provision, faithfulness, and love from Boaz. Of course, these blessings had their true origin in God; Boaz was simply the channel through whom they arrived.

Yes, your blessings may come *through* a man or a woman, but the key word is *through*. Other people are often the channels that God uses to get His blessings to us. But the "Boaz blessing" comes from the Lord. Just because Ruth married the "channel" God had used to deliver her blessings doesn't mean you will marry yours, too. God has many channels. Rest assured that He will connect you with the right ones once you have stepped into the proper season—not before, and not in a position other than what He has ordained.

Practice Patience while Awaiting Your "Suddenly"

I love strawberries. They taste best when they're in season. Here in Virginia, we have a Strawberry Festival every May, in the middle of prime strawberry season. You can get just about anything made out of strawberries at the festival, and it's all delicious.

Just like strawberries in May, you will bear the best fruit for God's kingdom in the middle of your season, and your fruit will ripen into a beautiful, bountiful harvest in God's perfect time. Strawberries aren't too good in February. But, if I wait until their season, they taste wonderful!

Stop trying to rush God's season. Your fruit isn't ready yet. But, when it is, suddenly you will be thrust into your palace position. For now, focus on being a standard setter right where you are and allow the fruit of the Spirit to grow in your life.

Chapter 3: Trust in God's Timing

Points to Ponder

1. Have you ever rushed the arrival of a season in your life? What were the consequences?

2. Think about an instance when something happened according to a timing that was not your personal preference. In hindsight, can you identify what God may have had in mind when He was orchestrating this event?

3. Ruth received her "Boaz blessing" because she was in the right place at the right time, fulfilling the will of God. Have you ever interpreted something or someone as a "Boaz blessing," thinking that it was part of God's plan for you, only to find out that He had something else in mind? How can you attune your heart more closely to the will of God and sharpen your discernment?

4. Is there a place where God has told you He wants to position you, but you haven't yet arrived? What can you do to prepare yourself for His positioning so that you'll be fruitful once you get there?

Meditate on these Scriptures, speak them aloud, and commit them to memory:

You intended to harm me, but God intended it for good to accomplish what is now being done, the saving of many lives.   (Genesis 50:20)

"For my thoughts are not your thoughts, neither are your ways my ways," declares the LORD. "As the heavens are higher than the earth, so are my ways higher than your ways and my thoughts than your thoughts."
(Isaiah 55:8–9)

And we know that in all things God works for the good of those who love him, who have been called according to his purpose.   (Romans 8:28)

— 4 —

Prepare for the Palace

God has a special call on your life. There's a realm of His kingdom that needs a standard setter, and you're the one He wants. But you'll have to undergo a process of preparation to get there, just as Esther had to do at the palace.

Jeremiah 1:4–5 says, *"The word of the LORD came to me, saying, 'Before I formed you in the womb I knew you, before you were born I set you apart; I appointed you as a prophet to the nations.'"* First, God knew Jeremiah; second, He formed him; and, third, He set Jeremiah apart according to His purpose for his life—in his case, to be a prophet. It was only after Jeremiah had been set apart that God appointed Him to fulfill His purpose.

The same three-step process happens in our lives. In other words, God first knew us in His heart—He knew what He wanted us to do in His kingdom—and then He formed us for that very purpose. Because God knew us first, He then formed us with every gift, every talent, every love, every desire, and every personality trait that we would need to fulfill His purpose for our lives.

We won't fulfill that purpose automatically, however. We were born sinners, remember? The Holy Spirit has a lot of work to do in our hearts and our minds to prepare us for our divine destinies. The key to

> The Holy Spirit has a lot of work to do in our hearts and our minds to prepare us for our divine destinies. The key to qualifying is to submit to the preparation process.

qualifying is to submit to the preparation process. Each of us must be qualified if we hope to make our appointment with our destiny.

Jeremiah went all the steps so he reached his scheduled appointment with his destiny. He was not only appointed as a prophet to the nations, but he reached his scheduled appointment on time and he fulfilled his purpose because he was fully prepared.

Go the Steps

I did a teaching series several years ago that I titled "No One Takes the Elevator; Everyone Takes the Steps." In this series, I talked about how everyone likes to get on the elevator, push the button, and arrive at the top! We like to do this in every area of our lives, not just when we are in an office building with thirty-plus floors. Not many people take the steps these days. Even though all of us could use the exercise, we don't have time for it. We are in a rush to get where we are going, only to rush off to the next place.

This has become a part of our culture, and we have adopted this type of action in all areas of our lives. When we get sick, we want to pop a pill and feel better immediately. If we are unhappy with our weight and want to lose a few pounds, we want to pop a different pill that allows us to eat anything we want to eat and still lose weight without any physical exercise. We go through the drive-through and we don't even have time to give the details of our order, so we just say, "I'll take a number three combo, please."

Everything is fast—we want it now, and now means immediately! We don't even want to wait on God and His timing. We like to help Him out so we can move things along a little bit—not smart! God never needs our help; He needs only our obedience.

The desire to "take the elevator" has become a part of our lives in every area. We want to start in the ministry, push a button, and arrive at the top. We want our business to clip along from floor to floor, or level to level, with ease and arrive at the top of the Fortune 500 list in no time. We want our relationships to be easy, and if we have to put any time into "working" through things, we just move on to another one. But no one takes the elevator; everyone is required to take the steps in all areas of life.

The steps are a setup from the Lord—a setup to be a build-up! He wants to build the character of Christ in us and that is learned only by going the "steps." My daughter has been a part of my ministry since she was in my womb. Throughout the years, I have seen her develop a great desire to be a part of various levels of leadership. I can remember when she longed to have the position of our receptionist. She just thought it would be so cool to answer the phones all day long. When she grew up, she wanted to be the receptionist at Joy Ministries; that was her dream position. She would beg me to allow her to answer the phones. So, finally, when she was about ten years old, we started allowing her to answer the switchboard after 5:00 p.m. She was so excited! She would sit (not so patiently) and wait for the phone to ring.

It didn't take long for her to realize that most of our calls came in before 5:00 p.m., so she started requesting to answer them beginning at 4:00 p.m. After about a year, we allowed her to answer calls before 5:00 p.m. And today, she is one of the most effective counselors in our phone center.

Not only does she answer phones; she also runs a summer camp for our children in our adopted neighborhoods. She is going the steps, and, as a result, she is becoming a very valuable player on our ministry team.

I believe that everybody needs to go the steps. I believe we do people a disservice if we just throw them into a top position. Actually we can set them up to fail or even to fall in their relationship with the Lord if we do. I have seen it time and time again, when a famous personality gives his life to the Lord, and the body of Christ promotes him to a place when he hasn't had the time to grow in his relationship with the Lord and thus grow in the character of Christ.

Just as my daughter has literally "grown up" in the ministry one step at a time, we must "grow up" in our palace, or the position that the Lord has called us to, and that takes time. It's during this time that we are going the steps that the Lord develops our character and works His character in us.

God sets us up for character development before His appointed time for promotion in our lives. And, it's important that we "go the steps" in the development of our character. If we don't "go the steps," we can trip up in our walk with the Lord and come falling down.

Joseph Went the Steps

Standard setters have the favor of God. Standard setters are blessed in whatever they put their hand to. Everyone around a standard setter is blessed because the standard setter affects the entire atmosphere by his presence. His presence brings the presence of the Lord and the favor of God. Those around the standard setter get to enjoy that blessing.

> *The LORD was with Joseph and he prospered, and he lived in the house of his Egyptian master. When his master saw that the LORD was with him and that the LORD gave him success in everything he did, Joseph found favor in his eyes and became his attendant. Potiphar put him in charge of his household, and he entrusted to his care everything he owned. From the time he put him in charge of his household and of all that he owned, the LORD blessed the household of the Egyptian because of Joseph. The blessing of the LORD was on everything Potiphar had, both in the house and in the field.* (Genesis 39:2–5)

Potiphar and everything that pertained to him was blessed because of the blessing that was on Joseph's life. Joseph had the favor and blessing of God upon him because he had godly character. Joseph went the steps—he went from the pit to slavery to the prison and finally landed in the palace. Through all the steps, Joseph grew and maintained a right heart attitude and godly character in all that he did. As a result, he became a standard setter.

When given the opportunity to sin, Joseph refused. When faced with temptation, Joseph held to his standards. When falsely accused even after he passed the temptation test, Joseph maintained his standards and as a result the blessing of the Lord was on him wherever he went.

> *So [Potiphar] left in Joseph's care everything he had; with Joseph in charge, he did not concern himself with anything except the food he ate. Now Joseph was well built and handsome, and after a while his master's wife took notice of Joseph and said, "Come to bed with me!" But he refused. "With me in charge," he told her, "my master does not concern himself with anything in the house; everything he owns he has entrusted to my care. No one is greater in this house than I am. My master has withheld nothing from me except you, because you are his wife. How then could I do such a wicked thing and sin against God? And though she spoke to Joseph day after day, he refused to go to bed with her or even be with her."* (Genesis 39:6–10)

Now, that's what I call a standard setter! The woman kept trying to talk Joseph into sinning day after day, and he refused to even hang around her. He didn't even want to be around her. Sin is repulsive to a standard setter. Standard setters lead the way—they set the example. They don't wait for others to lead the way. They jump out in front and lead by example. And when others around them display a standard contrary to theirs, they hold their ground.

They have unshakable, immovable standards that represent who they are and what they stand for, no matter what situation they find themselves in.

A few verses later, we read that Joseph was falsely accused of the very sin he had refused to commit and then thrown into prison. Even behind bars, the Lord was with him and granted him favor with the prison warden. Even in prison, Joseph was put in charge.

Standard setters always rise to the top, no matter what situation they find themselves in. The Lord was with Joseph and gave him success in whatever he did. (See Genesis 39:23.) The prison was actually a direct route to the palace for Joseph. Unlike others, standard setters always reach their final destination. The Word tells us that many are called but few are chosen. (See Matthew 22:14 NKJV.) The chosen ones, the people the Lord selects for the job, are the standard setters.

> Standard setters always rise to the top, no matter what situation they find themselves in.

Your Steps Are Ordered by the Lord

I believe that many of you are about to step into what God has for you. Many of you are about to step into a new level. Many of you are about to step into a long-awaited victory after an intense time of battle or struggle. The key word here is *step*. You arrive at your destination only after you've gone the steps, one step of obedience at a time. You step into your victory because you have gone the steps. You step into your ministry because you have gone the steps. You step into the best business opportunity of your life because you have gone the steps.

Most people who don't go the steps become shooting stars that eventually fall right out of sight. God's plan is to take you through all the steps—one at a time—because He loves you so much that He wants to set you up for success. As you submit to each step of preparation He takes you through, you will successfully reach your destination in the Lord. Everything is already in place; you just need to step into it—one step of obedience at a time.

Let the Lord Determine Your Steps

Determination can be a very good thing if we apply our determination in the direction of the Holy Spirit's leading. As a young Christian, I told the Lord that I didn't see how He could use me because I didn't think I had any gifts. I saw singing and playing the piano as the main gifts, and I did not have either one of them. Several years later, the Lord told me that I had the gift of determination. He went on to say that He had given me just what I needed to fulfill the call of God on my life.

The Lord began to ask me questions. He said, "Do you remember when your dad said he wasn't going to pay for your college, but you were determined to go anyway?" I said, "Yes." He said, "Do you remember when people were telling you that women couldn't be preachers, but you obeyed My voice, anyway?" I said, "Yes." He continued with a list of questions asking me if I remembered this and if I remembered that. I kept answering "Yes," and He said, "That's because I gave you the gift of determination. I gave you the very gift that you would need to fulfill the call I have on your life."

Well, I'd never thought that determination was a gift. But as I answered all the questions, I came to realize that if I didn't have Holy Ghost determination, I would have taken that government job right out of high school and I would probably still be sitting in my office typing letters.

There is always blessing on the other side of obedience. When God told me to move thirteen hours away from my family and go to college, I really didn't feel like going. Later, when the Lord told me to move to Virginia Beach and go to graduate school, it was the last thing that I wanted to do. I wanted to stay in Cleveland, Tennessee, and establish a base for my evangelistic ministry and go "save the world." When my husband left me with a two-week-old baby girl, I wanted to move back to my hometown, or anywhere as far away from Virginia Beach and all the painful memories as possible. But each time that I obeyed the Lord, great blessing awaited me.

As we allow the Lord to determine our steps, we will always be glad we did. Jesus said,

> *I tell you the truth,…no one who has left home or brothers or sisters or mother or father or children or fields for me and the gospel will fail to receive a hundred times as much in this present age (homes, brothers, sisters, mothers, children and fields—and with them, persecutions) and in the age to come, eternal life.*   (Mark 10:29–30)

In other words, God never asks us to give up something for Him for which He doesn't give us back something much better. He wants to determine our steps because He wants to bring us into the best place possible!

The Steps Test Your Faith

The whole point in our taking the steps is to test our faith and develop our character—kingdom character, as I like to call it.

James 1:2–4 says, *"Consider it pure joy, my brothers, whenever you face trials of many kinds, because you know that the testing of your faith develops perseverance. Perseverance must finish its work so that you may be mature and complete, not lacking anything."*

I can remember the first time someone told me that God tests us. I was a young Christian, and I thought, *No way! God doesn't test us.* Oh, yes He does! He tests us in many areas, including our hearts and our faith. He takes us through tests of faith in order to develop our perseverance. We must have perseverance so we can continue doing whatever He has called us to do, despite any difficulties or opposition. We must persevere so we can be steadfast in our purpose. You learn perseverance on the steps! You don't learn perseverance in the elevator, believe me. People like to get in the elevator because they like to be elevated—it's a passive experience. People don't like to take the steps because it's a workout for their flesh—ouch!

James 1:3 says that *"you know that the testing of your faith develops perseverance."* In times of testing, God is just developing our perseverance so that we can be *"mature and complete, not lacking anything"* (verse 4). If we lack any Christlike character trait, we will never graduate to the next level.

> You don't learn perseverance in the elevator, believe me.

In college and in graduate school, I learned that I couldn't be even a half of a credit short if I wanted to graduate. The same is true in the school of the Spirit. We must be mature and complete in our character, not lacking even a single credit, not failing a final exam, in order to graduate to the next level.

God loves us so much that He won't allow us to graduate to the next level if He knows we aren't prepared to pass the tests that await us there. He always wants to set us up to succeed. When we are fruitful and successful, we bring the Father glory!

You Receive All the Promises by Faith

The testing of our faith is so important because without faith, no one can please the Lord. (See Hebrews 11:6.) And it is so important because we receive all the promises of God for our life by faith.

Romans 4:13 says, *"It was not through law that Abraham and his offspring received the promise that he would be heir of the world, but through the righteousness that comes by faith."*

When we live by faith, we are doing the righteous thing, or the "right" thing. That's why the growth of our faith through testing is so important! If you pass the test, you graduate to the next level. If you are never tested, you can never be evaluated and then promoted.

God isn't moved by our emotions or our wills; He's moved by our faith. I can remember one night lying in bed crying and begging God to answer my prayer. As I prayed, I basically unloaded my emotions, telling God why He had to do this certain thing for me. Well, it's not wrong to pour out our hearts to the Lord; we should allow ourselves to cry and get it out. But I was trying to move God by my emotions, and I didn't realize it. After I was done with my emotional plea, the Lord said, "Danette, I'm not moved by your emotions. I'm moved by your faith."

Yes, God is a God of compassion, and He's often moved by our distress. But my emotional plea didn't stir up the compassion I was attempting to get. I finally snapped out of my "pity-party prayer" and started praying in faith. That's when I saw results!

When we pray in faith, we pray the Word over our situation. When we pray in emotions, we can easily begin to pray out of fear and not out of faith.

If we don't go the steps and allow our faith to be developed, we'll be left with only ourselves to have faith in—and that guarantees failure.

The Promise of Hope

Psalm 33:16–17 says, *"No king is saved by the size of his army; no warrior escapes by his great strength. A horse is a vain hope for deliverance; despite all its great strength it cannot save."* Honey, it's a sad day when you go to battle with your hope in your horse instead of in your God. I've been there, done that, and I wouldn't advise it for anyone. All horses are "vain hopes" during times of trouble or on the day of battle. If your hope is in your paycheck, your friends, or your bank account—anything other than the Lord—the day will come when you'll lose hope. But if your hope is in the Lord, and if you trust Him every step of the way, you will always come out on top.

Romans 15:13 says, *"May the God of hope fill you with all joy and peace as you trust in him, so that you may overflow with hope by the power of the Holy Spirit."* As we go the steps, it teaches us to have our hope in the right place. Our hope must be in the Lord and in the Lord alone. The world needs hope like never before. As Christians, we are supposed to "overflow" with hope by the power of the Holy Spirit. If we don't have our hope in the right place, there won't be any flow of hope in our lives to "overflow" to others. Don't get yourself into a place where you have a hope drought. We must keep our hope flowing by the power of the Holy Spirit. Then, and only then, will we be filled with joy and peace because we are trusting in Him.

The Promise of Fruit

Gifts are given, but fruit is grown, and the same is true in our walk with the Lord. God has freely given us all gifts, but the fruit of the Spirit must be grown in our lives. Fruit doesn't grow overnight. Did you ever plant seeds as a child? If you were like me, you woke up every morning and ran to check and see whether they had sprouted or grown. I used to check the cup two or three times a day to see if my plants had grown. I was so impatient in waiting for the growth process, I would actually stick my finger in the soil from time to time to see if I could find the seed. I wanted to make sure everything was all right.

Just as there are stages or steps in the growth process when you plant a seed, we have to take the steps in order for our "plants"—the fruit of the Spirit—to grow in our lives, so that we can set a standard in this generation. God works fruit in us, often through other people, through trials, and through challenging times. These are the steps of our journey as we walk with and grow in the Lord.

Chapter 4: Prepare for the Palace

Points to Ponder

1. Think about an area in which you are impatient to improve and would rather take the "elevator" than the "steps." What are the specific steps that are required?

2. If you were to undertake those steps, would you be better prepared for the desired position? How so?

3. What are some of the unique gifts God has given you? Are you putting them to use in His kingdom? If not, pray and ask God to show you which skills He would have you develop. Also consider asking someone you know well to identify any skills and aptitudes you may have but are not putting to use.

4. Have you ever experienced a trial or hardship that you later recognized as a test from God? What particular character quality (or qualities) did it help you to develop?

Meditate on these Scriptures, speak them aloud, and commit them to memory:

We have different gifts, according to the grace given us.　(Romans 12:6)

And without faith it is impossible to please God, because anyone who comes to him must believe that he exists and that he rewards those who earnestly seek him.　　　　　　　　　　　　　　(Hebrews 11:6)

Consider it pure joy, my brothers, whenever you face trials of many kinds, because you know that the testing of your faith develops perseverance. Perseverance must finish its work so that you may be mature and complete, not lacking anything.　　　　　　　　　　　　　(James 1:2–4)

PART TWO

PASS THE TESTS

— 5 —

FAVOR: THE KEY TO PROMOTION

When the king's order and edict had been proclaimed, many girls were brought to the citadel of Susa and put under the care of Hegai. Esther also was taken to the king's palace and entrusted to Hegai, who had charge of the harem. The girl pleased him and won his favor. Immediately he provided her with her beauty treatments and special food. He assigned to her seven maids selected from the king's palace and moved her and her maids into the best place in the harem....And Esther won the favor of everyone who saw her. (Esther 2:8–9, 15)

Favor is the unfolding theme illustrated throughout the entire book of Esther. It's no wonder that the favor that was on Esther's life brought her step-by-step to the palace and to her destiny in God. From the minute she entered the palace, she was given the best. She was shown favor from the minute she arrived. She won favor with everyone, including the king.

Favor is the key to promotion, including the promotion that occurs when we qualify to be standard setters. So, the question is, what is favor, and how do we receive it? One definition of favor is simply approval. When you have God's stamp of approval, that's all you need. You and God are the majority. Everyone and everything can be against you, but if God is on your side, you are sure to win! You don't need the approval of man; you simply need the approval of God. When you have divine favor, every door that needs to be opened will be, everything you need to happen will happen, and everything you need shall be given to you, all because you have the favor and approval of God.

Of course, earning approval is not as simple as it sounds. Favor isn't automatic. As we will see, Esther found favor with the king first and foremost because of her humble, obedient heart. Once we have a firm foundation in the Lord, and once we go the steps to earn favor, we'll find our way to the palace.

Divine favor begins with a right relationship with the Lord. Proverbs 8:35 says, *"For whoever finds* [wisdom] *finds life and receives favor from the LORD."* To find wisdom, it is necessary to establish a relationship with the Lord that is both intimate and reverent, for *"the fear of the LORD is the beginning of wisdom, and knowledge of the Holy One is understanding"* (Proverbs 9:10), and we know from the previous verse that wisdom is the beginning of favor from God. All favor has its origins in a right relationship with God. If we do not have a right relationship with the Lord, we cannot obtain His favor. We may try to earn favor in our own strength, but that is a sure way to fail.

Favor Depends on Character

> When your character is pleasing to the Lord, His favor will propel you into any position the Father wants you in.

Remember what Ruth said to Boaz when he showered her with favor? *"You have given me comfort and have spoken kindly to your servant— though I do not have the standing of one of your servant girls"* (Ruth 2:13). She had neither position nor standing, but her outstanding character stood out to Boaz and earned her his favor, just as it had already earned her the favor of God.

When your character is pleasing to the Lord, His favor will propel you into any position the Father wants you in. At Joy Ministries, we have a program called Character Counts that we use in our outreaches to at-risk children and teenagers. This program is vital because if we can teach our children to have strong Christian character, we are setting them up to succeed in life. If they develop Christlike character, they will obtain the favor of God and succeed in all that they do. Character counts—a lot more than our gifts and talents, in fact!

Favor Transcends Typical Measures of Success

All promotion comes from God alone. Don't wear yourself out trying to receive promotion from a man, an organization, or a corporation. When God wants to promote you, nothing and no one can stop His promotion process. Esther 2:17 says, *"Now the king was attracted to Esther more than to any of the other women, and she won his favor and approval more than any of the other virgins."* When you have the favor of God, He will give you favor with man, as well, no matter his position. For *"even the heart of the king is in the hand of the LORD"* (Proverbs 21:1).

When our hearts are right, when we are living out standards of godly character, we have the Lord's favor and blessing. Don't look for a man or a woman to open doors for you. Don't look to a man or a woman to promote you. God will open the doors to His perfect will for you, and He will bring promotion. Meanwhile, you must focus on growing in godly character. As you live a lifestyle that pleases the Father, His favor on your life will open the door to His best. As we simply do our part, the Lord will be faithful to do His part, in His perfect timing.

God prepares us right where we are. Sometimes, we think if we aren't currently furthering our education at a well-known institution, we aren't being prepared for God's promotion in our lives. Don't buy that lie! Divine favor transcends education, social status, economic standing, and every other standard of comparison. My degree from the Master is much more valuable than my master's degree from Regent University. When you graduate and get your degree from the Master, you have passed the test, and you're about to be blessed.

Favor Transcends Age and Physical Stature

The Lord prepared little David to do a great big job. A job that was so big that the "big boys" didn't want to do it. David's preparation didn't come the way you would expect. He never graduated from Yale or Harvard. He wasn't even prepared the same way the "big boys" were. Yet, he received his preparation simply from doing what he was given to do at the place where he was instructed to do it.

First Samuel 16:1 says, *"The LORD said to Samuel, 'How long will you mourn for Saul, since I have rejected him as king over Israel? Fill your horn with oil and be on your way; I am sending you to Jesse of Bethlehem. I have chosen one of his sons to be king.'"*

If you'll recall, Saul had lost his position because of his disobedience. He did not do everything the Lord told him to do. He feared man and did not fear God. As a result, the Lord was about to anoint the next king. But everyone was surprised at God's choice.

> *Jesse had seven of his sons pass before Samuel, but Samuel said to him, "The LORD has not chosen these." So he asked Jesse, "Are these all the sons you have?" "There is still the youngest," Jesse answered, "but he is tending the sheep." Samuel said, "Send for him; we will not sit down until he arrives."*   (1 Samuel 16:10–11)

I can imagine that Jesse was proud as he paraded all of his sons—well, the sons he thought to be likely candidates for king—before Samuel. Yet, as each one stood before him, Samuel received no confirmation from God. None of them was His choice.

After seven different sons paraded by, I can imagine that both Jesse and Samuel were wondering what was going on. You see, little David wasn't even in the running! His father had dismissed him as a possibility because of his youth and his small stature.

Samuel finally asked Jesse, "Are you sure these are *all* of your sons?" He may have even begun to doubt if he was hearing correctly from the Lord.

God loves to shower His favor upon the people whom nobody even considers. Little David was on the back side of the desert just tending a "few little sheep." He was the youngest, he was the smallest, he was the least likely, yet he had found favor with the Lord, and so the Lord called for him and raised him up to serve in a specific capacity.

> *So he sent and had him brought in. He was ruddy, with a fine appearance and handsome features. Then the LORD said, "Rise and anoint him; he is the one." So Samuel took the horn of oil and anointed him in the presence of his brothers, and from that day on the Spirit of the LORD came upon David in power. Samuel then went to Ramah.*   (1 Samuel 16:12–13)

The Lord said, "Rise and anoint him; he is the one!" I believe the Lord is saying to you today, "Rise up! You are the one! I have called you for such a time as this!" You may be the least likely, but so was Esther, and so was David. Little David had been trained and equipped. Little David had proven himself faithful over a few small sheep. And so, in His perfect timing, the Lord anointed him and used him for an important job that only little David could do—defeat the giant.

David said to the Philistine, "You come against me with sword and spear and javelin, but I come against you in the name of the LORD Almighty, the God of the armies of Israel, whom you have defied. This day the LORD will hand you over to me, and I'll strike you down and cut off your head. Today I will give the carcasses of the Philistine army to the birds of the air and the beasts of the earth, and the whole world will know that there is a God in Israel." (1 Samuel 17:45–46)

David was fighting for the glory of God. He was in the right place at the right time, doing the right thing, with the right heart. As a result, he had the favor of God on all that he did. We must be ready and willing to lay down our lives for the purposes of the Lord. If we do, we will find favor with God and rise to set a standard in His kingdom, just as Esther and David did.

> Are you the least likely for promotion? Then, get excited—in God's book, you rank up there with David and Esther!

David started out as an unassuming shepherd boy and ended up being the greatest king in Israel's history. With the favor of God on your side, you, too, can beat the odds and defy everyone's expectations. Are you the least likely for promotion? Then, get excited—in God's book, you rank up there with David and Esther!

Favor Transcends Pits and Problems

It may be tempting to think that the people God anoints and uses have never been through any hardships. I'm sure there are people who flip through the channels, see my television program, and think I have never been through a test or trial. But those who stop and watch, even for just a few minutes, know the truth: I've been through my share of "pits" in life, including a broken home, divorce, and financial struggles, and yet, because I had the favor of God, I made it out of each of them.

Again, Esther was an ordinary girl; the only thing "extraordinary" about her was the hardship she had endured. Like Esther, most of us have been through many "pits." The key is not to lose God's favor by getting bitter and refusing to forgive those who have hurt us. If we "park in the pit" and decide to live there, we will forgo God's favor and miss out on God's purpose for our lives—a purpose that can put our "pits" to good use!

Joseph, another standard setter in the Bible whom we've discussed several times, was caught in a literal pit, thanks to his scheming brothers, and then sold into slavery. But he recognized that God can use our pits to promote us! Years later, against all odds, he attained a high position in the palace. When he was reunited with his brothers, he told them, *"You intended to harm me, but God intended it for good to accomplish what is now being done, the saving of many lives"* (Genesis 50:20).

No matter what particular "pit" you're in right now, God has a purpose for it. *"'For I know the plans I have for you,' declares the LORD, 'plans to prosper you and not to harm you, plans to give you hope and a future'"* (Jeremiah 29:11).

Even in the midst of seemingly impossible circumstances, when you have the favor of God, you'll make it through unscathed. Focus on His favor and don't allow the pain of the past or the present to stifle your future.

Esther wasn't raised in the ideal situation. She didn't have a picture-perfect life. But she had the favor of God, and that was enough. He watched over her in every situation and brought her out on top.

Favor Transcends False Accusation and Personal Attacks

The favor of God follows us, even when others treat us with anything but favor. Again, Joseph was a man of God who maintained godly character in spite of all he went through—being falsely accused by his own brothers and thrown into a pit, only to be sold into slavery. Later on, he ascended to a high position of authority in Potiphar's palace, only to be thrown into prison because of more false accusations, this time from the lips of Potiphar's wife.

It's always hardest to hear false accusations from those who are close to us, because we feel a deep sense of betrayal. The psalmist captured this well in Psalm 55:

> *If an enemy were insulting me, I could endure it; if a foe were raising himself against me, I could hide from him. But it is you, a man like myself, my companion, my close friend, with whom I once enjoyed sweet fellowship as we walked with the throng at the house of God.*   (verses 12–14)

The closer the relationship, the more severe the pain of that offense will be. But when you have the favor of God, you know that your reaction determines your destiny. Choose to forgive those who have wounded you, and remember that God's esteem is all that counts.

In spite of the false accusations and slander voiced against him, Joseph was supernaturally propelled forward into his God-given purpose, all because of favor.

Joseph's master took him and put him in prison, the place where the king's prisoners were confined. But while Joseph was there in the prison, the LORD was with him; he showed him kindness and granted him favor in the eyes of the prison warden. (Genesis 39:20–21)

Because Joseph had quality character, he reached an all-time high level of favor—while he was in prison for a crime he never committed, I might add.

God was strategically positioning him once again for his own palace, or his unique purpose in God. While in prison, Joseph interpreted the dreams of the chief cupbearer to the king. Joseph told him, "When all goes well with you, remember me." Joseph wanted the cupbearer to mention his name to Pharaoh. But instead, the cupbearer forgot all about Joseph. *So much for favor,* he might have been thinking.

People may forget about you and what you have done for them, but God never forgets us. If you have done what you have done as unto the Lord, then God will never forget about you. That's exactly what happened to Joseph— God remembered him at the appointed time!

Two full years passed, and then, one night, Pharaoh had a dream, and everything changed. Remember our discussion about "suddenlies"? Well, the chief cupbearer suddenly remembered Joseph and his knack for interpreting dreams.

Genesis 41:14 says, *"So Pharaoh sent for Joseph, and he was quickly brought from the dungeon. When he had shaved and changed his clothes, he came before Pharaoh."* Even though the preparation process may have seemed slow, suddenly Joseph was brought before the king. Quickly Joseph was brought from the dungeon—the dungeon! God will bring you to the forefront from the dungeon, from the backside of the desert like little David, or from out of obscurity like Esther. But when God wants to put you out in the forefront, God can put you out in the forefront overnight! And that's just what happened to Joseph.

Joseph had to quickly shave and change his clothes. He had to get dressed and ready for where he was going—before the king. I want to encourage you today! If you have been through a season of false accusations, hang on, because promotion is just ahead. Keep your heart right. Rest on Isaiah 54:17: *"No weapon forged against you will prevail, and you will refute every tongue that accuses you. This is the heritage of the servants of the LORD, and this is their vindication from me,' declares the LORD."*

> The King of Kings is about to summon you. He has called you and positioned you for such a time as this!

Keep your focus and remember the favor of God on your life. Get dressed and ready, because the King of Kings is about to summon you. He has called you and positioned you for such a time as this!

Favor Is Waiting for You to Ask

In many cases, we don't have favor because we don't ask for it. We don't ask God, and we don't ask man. Favor is just waiting for you to ask.

At Joy Ministries, we organize more than twenty local outreaches in low-income housing areas. We have adopted about ten subsidized neighborhoods where we serve on a regular basis. Local businesses and churches are familiar with our work and have been a great source of support over the years. We have a large operating budget to fund these outreaches, but we rely 100 percent on donations, which, as you know, requires fund-raising.

A few years ago, I made a phone call to a local business owner, hoping he would agree to make a donation toward one of our upcoming outreaches. As I prepared to call him, I kept thinking, *I don't really feel like asking him for money. I hope he doesn't get upset that I'm calling again.* When he picked up the phone and found out who I was, he said, "I was wondering when you were going to call me. It took you long enough! I have some money for you." I didn't even have to ask—he had been waiting to give me money.

Favor is just waiting for us to ask. God had given me such favor with this businessman. Don't allow the enemy to talk you out of asking. Favor is just waiting for you to ask!

Ask and it will be given to you; seek and you will find; knock and the door will be opened to you. For everyone who asks receives; he who seeks finds; and to him who knocks, the door will be opened. (Matthew 7:7–8)

Favor is just waiting for you to ask, seek, and knock. Seasons of life change, but God's favor never does. His favor on our lives just grows as it follows us into each new season. When you have clear focus, the change of season doesn't bother or shake you.

Pass the Tests and Be Blessed

To help us develop character and ultimately earn favor, which is our key to the palace, God takes us through a series of tests. As we pass each one, we're promoted to the next level, climbing ever closer to our palace position. These tests will assess our humility, our obedience, our integrity, and our beauty—spiritual beauty, that is. If we don't pass on the first try, God loves us so much that He allows us to retake the test as many times as needed until we pass with flying colors.

Take the children of Israel, for example. They were tested in the wilderness, and it took them forty *years* to pass the test. Some of them even died trying. Let's make sure we submit to the preparation process and learn quickly! Get ready to pass the test and be blessed as a standard setter in God's kingdom.

Chapter 5: Favor: The Key to Promotion

Points to Ponder

1. Have you ever been in a situation in which you would have failed if it weren't for God's favor? What did you learn from that situation, and did it help you in future experiences?

2. Favor depends on character. What are some key character traits that are pleasing to the Lord and attract His favor?

3. Of the traits you listed in your response to the previous question, which ones are lacking the most in your life? What steps can you take to develop them?

Meditate on these Scriptures, speak them aloud, and commit them to memory:

"For I know the plans I have for you," declares the LORD, "plans to prosper you and not to harm you, plans to give you hope and a future."

(Jeremiah 29:11)

For surely, O LORD, you bless the righteous; you surround them with your favor as with a shield. (Psalm 5:12)

Ask and it will be given to you; seek and you will find; knock and the door will be opened to you. For everyone who asks receives; he who seeks finds; and to him who knocks, the door will be opened. (Matthew 7:7–8)

— 6 —

THE TEST OF HUMILITY

During the time Mordecai was sitting at the king's gate, Bigthana and Teresh, two of the king's officers who guarded the doorway, became angry and conspired to assassinate King Xerxes. But Mordecai found out about the plot and told Queen Esther, who in turn reported it to the king, giving credit to Mordecai. (Esther 2:21–22)

Because of her heart of humility, Esther was prepared for greatness long before she reached the palace. This rare trait made her teachable and obedient throughout every step of her preparation process, so that, when her preparations were complete, she was ready to be ushered into the place of honor the Lord had ordained for her. Her humility came across at the palace, where she gave credit to Mordecai for uncovering the plot against the king instead of taking the credit for herself.

In God's kingdom, a lot of what we learn in the secular world is reversed. To go up, you must go down: *"For whoever exalts himself will be humbled, and whoever humbles himself will be exalted"* (Matthew 23:12). While society exalts self-promotion and prideful striving, true standard setters have hearts of humility.

Don't Despise Humble Beginnings

Proverbs 15:33 says, *"The fear of the LORD teaches a man wisdom, and humility comes before honor."* Humility comes before honor, and the humility in Esther's heart preexisted her rise to a place of honor in the palace. Esther's humble beginnings actually served as a place of great preparation, further proof that God truly does work all things together for the good of those who love Him and respond obediently to His call. (See Romans 8:28.)

The truth is that no one starts at the top, so we shouldn't despise small beginnings. (See Zechariah 4:10.) God loves to do big things with small resources. The bigger His plans for you, the "smaller" you will probably start out. When I started my television ministry, God told me to use what I had and warned me not to let pride get in the way. So, I hung a blue bed sheet on my living room wall, and my television ministry began.

> If we're going to be standard setters, we shouldn't insist on starting big. Instead, we ought to minister "big" at the bottom.

If we're going to be standard setters, we shouldn't insist on starting big. Instead, we ought to minister "big" at the bottom, no matter how lowly our position, and trust that God will lift us in due time.

Components of True Humility

As we seek to develop humble hearts, we need to make sure that our humility is authentic. False humility doesn't fool God, and it doesn't get us anywhere. When our humility isn't genuine, we try really hard to act humble, but pride remains written all over our faces. So, let's talk about the aspects of true humility—the kind God honors and rewards.

Compassion

A heart of true humility is characterized by great compassion, which often comes after we've gone through particularly difficult circumstances. I can imagine that Esther took a lot of compassion to the palace. She had suffered a great deal, having lost both of her parents at an early age, and I'm sure that her troubles were not limited to being orphaned. But the experience would have softened her heart to other orphans, as well as to anyone suffering the pain of personal loss.

My daughter lost her father when she was only four years old. It was not a loss she recovered from quickly. Yet the experience of losing her father first to divorce and then to death created a deep compassion in her heart for hurting people. She has a special love for children being raised in broken homes and dealing with difficult situations.

Since she was very young, she has had a heart to minister to children in orphanages in the United States and overseas. Her heart goes out to children who don't have a mom or a dad—or both. When she compares herself to children with no parents at all, she feels grateful to have a mom—and a great mom, at that!—but the comparison does not puff her up with pride. Instead, it increases her passion for helping orphans and showing God's love to them.

It is true that people sometimes lose their compassion after obtaining a high position or achieving a longtime goal. But Esther never lost her compassion, even when she'd made it to the palace. She had a heart of compassion for her people and determined to fight for their lives instead of growing complacent.

Absence of Self-Serving Agendas

When Esther made it to the palace, her mission was far from accomplished. It would have been easy to sit back and say, "I'm a queen now, so I might as well enjoy the pleasures of royalty. Too bad for those poor Jews." No! She wasn't above humbling herself in order to help the people—*her* people, the Jewish commoners. She didn't use her elevated role as a shield to protect herself while the rest of the Jews perished according to Haman's plan. With a heart of true humility, Esther made the Jews' agenda—life preservation, in essence—her own and committed to seeing it fulfilled at all costs.

Esther 7:3–4 says, *"Then Queen Esther answered, 'If I have found favor with you, O king, and if it pleases your majesty, grant me my life—this is my petition. And spare my people—this is my request.'"*

The king said to Esther, "I'll give you whatever you want, even up to half of the kingdom." (See Esther 7:2.) Talk about favor! Had we been in Esther's position, we might have listed off the things we wanted most—a new car, a weeklong shopping spree, and the like. But not Esther! In a spirit of humility, she prioritized the interests of her people. Her heart of humility paved the way for an entire nation to be saved. What character!

Yet, because of her humility, Esther did not take him up on his offer for her personal gain. Instead, she used her position in the palace to benefit her people.

A Teachable Spirit

Esther 2:15 says, *"When the turn came for Esther…to go to the king, she asked for nothing other than what Hegai, the king's eunuch who was in charge of the harem, suggested. And Esther won the favor of everyone who saw her."*

Humble hearts gain great wisdom because they are easily teachable. With humility comes a teachable heart, and with a teachable heart comes great wisdom. Psalm 25:9 says, *"He guides the humble in what is right and teaches them his way."*

Prideful people, on the other hand, are very difficult to teach. They think they know it all. It amazes me how so many teenagers, in particular, presume to know it all. Many of them act like their parents were born yesterday and don't know anything. And I was no different—until I went away to college and finally realized how smart my mom really was. It was during those years that I remembered all the things she had taught me. And, much to my surprise, she had always been right. I can remember thinking, *Wow. We are paying all of this money for me to go to college and get smart, but I'm really learning how smart my mom really is and must have been all along!*

Let's try to avoid being spiritual "teenagers" who claim to know everything. The truth was, the more education I received, the more I realized I really didn't know a lot at all. I can remember graduating with my master's degree; everyone was impressed with my accomplishments and those of my classmates. But at that time, it was more obvious to me than ever that I still had a whole lot to learn.

> Let's try to avoid being spiritual "teenagers" who claim to know everything.

The truth is, we will always have a lot to learn. If we keep our hearts humble and teachable, God will fill us with His truth and wisdom as we progress forward to our position in the "palace."

The Holy Spirit will teach us all things, but we have to be teachable in order to learn. If we aren't humble, no one can teach us—not even God!

Consistent Prayer

We read in James 4:6 that God *"opposes the proud but gives grace to the humble."* When you choose humility, God rewards you with His grace, which exceeds any human recognition we could earn by rejecting humility and going after self-exaltation.

Abraham is a good example of someone who was blessed because of his humility, which came across perhaps most profoundly in the way that he sought God's wisdom for every move he made, rather than presuming to know what to do in his own intelligence. As a result, Abraham became the father of many nations. He knew his God-given purpose, but it was humility that earned him the grace to fulfill that purpose.

We read in Genesis 12:8 that Abraham *"went on toward the hills east of Bethel and pitched his tent.... There he built an altar to the LORD and called upon the name of the LORD."* Everywhere Abraham went, he built an altar. In other words, his life was filled with "altar experiences," or times when he met God in prayer. Abraham lived this type of lifestyle because he was humbly dependent upon the Lord.

Prayer is an act of humility when it shows that we are dependent upon the Lord. It doesn't take a lot of humility to pray when we are in the midst of a major storm. But it does take humility when we seek God on our every move and on our every decision.

A heart that isn't humble says, "I can handle this. I don't need God." What is your lifestyle saying today? Are you humbly dependent upon the Lord, or have you been depending upon yourself a little too much?

In 2 Chronicles 7:14, the Lord says, *"If my people, who are called by my name, will humble themselves and **pray** and **seek my face**..., then I will hear from heaven and will forgive their sin and will heal their land"* (emphasis added).

God changes things because of our humble dependence upon Him in prayer. He wants us to call on His name for the big things and the small things alike, because, when we do, we acknowledge that we can do nothing on our own.

Start as a Servant

I may have a master's degree, but I can honestly say that my degree from the Master, Jesus Christ, is of infinitely greater value, and I earned it in large part during the time I spent waitressing during my years of graduate school. As a waitress, I had to give the customers my best, even when my feet hurt, my back ached, and I was almost too tired to hold my head up. Serving in a restaurant disciplined me to smile, exude friendliness, and serve with excellence, no matter how big my tips.

It's one thing to be paid to serve in a restaurant, hotel, or other venue that specializes in hospitality. But a true servant sacrifices herself for no compensation whatsoever. And anyone who desires to be a standard setter in the kingdom of God must start as a servant.

We must have a servant's heart, and the best way to get one is to jump in and start serving. We can't serve when it's convenient and call ourselves servants. We can't just try to be what God wants us to be. We must become servants, taking on that identity for life. When you get into the habit of serving, your heart will begin to incline automatically to those in need. After a while, once your humble posture has stood the test of time, your identity will be confirmed as one of God's faithful servants.

God promotes faithful servants—those who humble themselves to serve others day after day, week after week, and year after year. We can't just serve for a day, a week, or a month and then expect our promotion to arrive. It's when we've served faithfully with the right attitude for a significant period of time that we pass the test of faithful servanthood and qualify for promotion.

The Blessings of Being a Servant

We have a striking example of a faithful servant in the story of Ruth, a young widow who chose to remain with her mother-in-law, Naomi, and serve her faithfully instead of trying to secure a new husband for herself. In Ruth's place, most women probably would not have chosen that path. Many of them might even have breathed a sigh of relief that they no longer had to put up with their mother-in-law! I know that's poor character, and I'm sure that would never be the case for you, but I still believe that Ruth's humble act of self-sacrifice is probably the exception to the rule.

Ruth the Moabitess said to Naomi, "Let me go to the fields and pick up the leftover grain behind anyone in whose eyes I find favor." Naomi said to her, "Go ahead, my daughter." So she went out and began to glean in the fields behind the harvesters. As it turned out, she found herself working in a field belonging to Boaz, who was from the clan of Elimelech. Just then Boaz arrived from Bethlehem and greeted the harvesters, "The LORD be with you!" "The LORD bless you!" they called back. Boaz asked the foreman of his harvesters, "Whose young woman is that?" The foreman replied, "She is the Moabitess who came back from Moab with Naomi. She said, 'Please let me glean and gather among the sheaves behind the harvesters.' She went into the field and has worked steadily from morning till now, except for a short rest in the shelter." So Boaz said to Ruth, "My daughter, listen to me. Don't go and glean in another field and don't go away from here. Stay here with my servant girls. Watch the field where the men are harvesting, and follow along after the girls. I have told the men not to touch you. And whenever you are thirsty, go and get a drink from the water jars the men have filled."   (Ruth 2:2–9)

Ruth's faithfulness in serving her mother-in-law got the attention of Boaz. When she asked him why he was showing her such favor, he replied, *"I've been told all about what you have done for your mother-in-law since the death of your husband—how you left your father and mother and your homeland and came to live with a people you did not know before. May the LORD repay you for what you have done"* (Ruth 2:11). Because Ruth humbled herself and committed to serving her mother-in-law, the Lord exalted her and blessed her beyond her greatest expectations. That's the way He always works when we follow the command of James 4:10: *"Humble yourselves before the Lord, and he will lift you up."*

When we humble ourselves and serve faithfully, it gets the attention of God. And He rewards His faithful servants! Not only was Ruth committed to serving her mother-in-law, but she was not above gleaning the leftovers. In other words, no act of service was beneath her. Ruth 2:3 says that she merely wanted to glean *behind* the harvesters. Little did she know that God was about to put her front and center! She wasn't going to be in the background for long. Ultimately, Ruth married Boaz and ended up owning the very field she had worked in so humbly.

Ruth received an even greater reward—one to last for all eternity. God honored Ruth's humility and faithful service by making her the grandmother of a king—King David (see Ruth 4:17)—and an ancestor of the King of Kings, the Lord Jesus Christ (see Isaiah 11.) Talk about a blessing!

Servants See Others through God's Eyes

Philippians 2:3–4 gives us the following instructions:

Do nothing out of selfish ambition or vain conceit, but in humility consider others better than yourselves. Each of you should look not only to your own interests, but also to the interests of others.

We should always be looking for ways to serve others. Esther had serving on her mind even when she reached the palace, and she demonstrated the ultimate trait of a servant: the willingness to lay down one's life for the sake of someone else. First John 3:16 says, *"This is how we know what love is: Jesus Christ laid down his life for us. And we ought to lay down our lives for our brothers."* Standard setters should be willing to do the same—to give it all for the sake of the gospel and for the purposes of God.

And the Greatest of These Is Love

It's hard to be humble if you don't love your neighbor as yourself, as Jesus commands in Luke 10:27. It takes God in our lives to really walk in love, because *"God is love"* (1 John 4:8). It's great to have faith and hope, of course, but those are worthless, as are all the acts of service we do, unless we're doing them out of love.

The apostle Paul made this point in his first letter to the Corinthians.

If I speak in the tongues of men and of angels, but have not love, I am only a resounding gong or a clanging cymbal. If I have the gift of prophecy and can fathom all mysteries and all knowledge, and if I have a faith that can move mountains, but have not love, I am nothing.
(1 Corinthians 13:1–2)

Even if we give everything we have to the poor, it doesn't mean much unless we do it in love. When God sends His Holy Spirit to dwell within us, we take on the nature of God, which is love. We can't walk in real love without God, because God Himself is love.

Dear friends, let us love one another, for love comes from God. Everyone who loves has been born of God and knows God. Whoever does not love does not know God, because God is love. (1 John 4:7–8)

Whoever does not love does not *really* know God. That's strong, but that's what the Word says. We may say we know God, but if we lack love—for our brothers and sisters, for our neighbors, for those we serve—we're living a lie.

When we hang out with the Holy Spirit, when we have fellowship with the Lord, we grow in our love walk. When we *really* know God, we take on His nature because we always become like the people we hang out with.

> When we *really* know God, we take on His nature because we always become like the people we hang out with.

Walking in love doesn't come automatically, though. We need the help of the Holy Spirit to develop the fruit of love in our lives and in our humble service to others.

In another of his epistles, the apostle Paul encouraged us to *"bear with each other and forgive whatever grievances you may have against one another....And over all these virtues put on love, which binds them all together in perfect unity"* (Colossians 3:13–14). We are to *"put on"* love as a garment, not "put on," or pretend, that we're walking in love. There's a lot of "putting on" going on! You may walk the walk and talk the talk, putting on the façade of love, but God knows when it's real. And His standard setters are clothed continually in the real thing.

Your love walk starts in your heart as you fellowship with the Holy Spirit. As we spend time with Him, He develops the heart of God in us—the heart of love.

Perhaps the best-known biblical explanation of love comes from the thirteenth chapter of Paul's first letter to the Corinthians. Let's see how it describes love and then apply its wisdom to our personal love walks.

> *Love endures long and is patient and kind; love never is envious nor boils over with jealousy, is not boastful or vainglorious, does not display itself haughtily. It is not conceited (arrogant and inflated with pride); it is not rude (unmannerly) and does not act unbecomingly. Love (God's love in us) does not insist on its own right or its own way, for it is not self-seeking; it is not touchy or fretful or resentful; it takes no account of the evil done to it (it pays no attention to a suffered wrong). It does not rejoice at injustice and unrighteousness, but rejoices when right and truth prevail. Love bears up under anything and everything that comes, is ever ready to believe the best of every person, its hopes are fadeless under all circumstances, and it endures everything (without weakening). Love never fails.*
>
> (1 Corinthians 13:4–8 AMP)

The first quality of love mentioned in 1 Corinthians 13 is patience: *"Love endures long and is patient"* (verse 4). Working on that quality alone gives us enough homework for a lifetime! Today, everything is instant; nobody can afford to wait. But God, in His infinite love for us, is infinitely patient with us. And we are to be patient with other people.

Next, love *"is kind"* (verse 4). Love expresses itself through our words, our attitudes, and even our nonverbal communication. Be careful what you convey with the rolling of your eyes and the smirk on your face.

Love *"is never envious nor boils over with jealousy"* (verse 4). In other words, love gets excited when other people are blessed and rejoices with them. Instead of envying others, get excited and say, "Thank You, Lord. I know I'm next in line for my miracle!"

Love *"is not boastful or vainglorious, does not display itself haughtily"* (verse 4). Boasting is the opposite of humility because it brandishes one's abilities and achievements in a manner that's intended to make others feel inferior or unworthy. When we boast about ourselves, we are not walking in love with our listeners or seeking to edify them.

Love *"is not conceited (arrogant and inflated with pride);...Love does not insist on its own rights or its own way, for it is not self-seeking..."* (verse 5). Love expresses itself in many ways, but the common denominator is giving, which seeks the good of others. Love gives forgiveness. Love gives preference to others. Love gives time, money, and attention. God showed His love for us by giving His one and only Son. (See John 3:16.)

Love *"is not touchy or fretful or resentful; it takes no account of the evil done to it [it pays no attention to a suffered wrong]"* (verse 5). In other words, love forgives easily and does not take offense!

If we don't walk in love, it grieves the Holy Spirit, not to mention makes it extremely difficult for us to practice humility as we discussed it in this chapter. A key characteristic of standard setters is a love walk that shines forth God's love to those around them and exhibits itself in acts of humility and service.

Ephesians 4:2 says, *"Be completely humble and gentle; be patient, bearing with one another in love."* Because Esther was completely humble, not just partially so, she passed the palace prep course. Once she arrived at her position, she remained patient and she walked in love with all of those around her. And we ought to do the same, by the equipping of God within us, because God is love.

Yes, God has called you to greatness. But God's definition of greatness is a lot different from the world's. Greatness, in God's eyes, is an attitude of humility, a spirit of servanthood, and a teachable heart filled with the love and character of Christ. If your God-ordained place of greatness puts you before the kings and queens of this world, well great. If it doesn't, it shouldn't matter, because you aren't striving for a position, anyway—right? What matters is faithfully doing all that God wants us to do in the place where He has positioned us. Now, that's greatness!

Chapter 6: The Test of Humility

Points to Ponder

1. Think about an experience that was particularly humbling for you. What was the particular type of pride you'd been exhibiting? (Spiritual pride? Intellectual pride? Pride in your social status, economic status, or ethnicity?)

2. How have you changed since then? In other words, have you deliberately worked toward developing humility in this particular area of your life? If you just now identified that area, what are some ways in which you can humble yourself in regard to it?

3. Jesus was the most humble Man who ever lived, but it's sometimes easier to emulate someone we can see and interact with. Do you know anyone who exhibits unusual humility? In what way(s) does this come across?

4. When was the last time you served someone (or a group of people) without any promise of compensation? How did it make you feel (a) about yourself and (b) about the people you served?

5. Review the apostle Paul's definition of love, as recorded in 1 Corinthians 13:4–8, and think of it as a checklist. Which aspect(s) are you exhibiting the best in your love walk? Which aspect(s) do you need to work on the most as you show love to God and others?

Meditate on these Scriptures, speak them aloud, and commit them to memory:

The fear of the LORD teaches a man wisdom, and humility comes before honor.   (Proverbs 15:33)

For whoever exalts himself will be humbled, and whoever humbles himself will be exalted.   (Matthew 23:12)

Do nothing out of selfish ambition or vain conceit, but in humility consider others better than yourselves. Each of you should look not only to your own interests, but also to the interests of others.   (Philippians 2:3–4)

This is how we know what love is: Jesus Christ laid down his life for us. And we ought to lay down our lives for our brothers.   (1 John 3:16)

Dear friends, let us love one another, for love comes from God. Everyone who loves has been born of God and knows God. Whoever does not love does not know God, because God is love.   (1 John 4:7–8)

— 7 —

THE PRIDE INDICATOR

On the seventh day, when King Xerxes was in high spirits from wine, he commanded the seven eunuchs who served him—Mehuman, Biztha, Harbona, Bigtha, Abagtha, Zethar and Carcas—to bring before him Queen Vashti, wearing her royal crown, in order to display her beauty to the people and nobles, for she was lovely to look at. But when the attendants delivered the king's command, Queen Vashti refused to come. Then the king became furious and burned with anger....[One of the nobles said,] "Therefore, if it pleases the king, let him issue a royal decree and let it be written in the laws of Persia and Media, which cannot be repealed, that Vashti is never again to enter the presence of King Xerxes. Also let the king give her royal position to someone else who is better than she. Then when the king's edict is proclaimed throughout all his vast realm, all the women will respect their husbands, from the least to the greatest." (Esther 1:10–12, 19–20)

We're going to take our focus off of Esther for a moment to consider Vashti, her predecessor. This is important to do because we don't want to make the same mistake Vashti did. When it comes down to it, Vashti was deposed because of pride—the arrogant attitude that caused her to defy her husband's wishes. Esther 1:12 says, *"But when the attendants delivered the king's command, Queen Vashti refused to come. Then the king became furious and burned with anger."* Yikes! You can't take pride to the palace, or you won't stay there for very long. Pride is the antithesis of humility, so, if we hope to pass the humility test, we have to fail the pride test—no pride must be found in us.

What happened to Vashti is a great illustration of Proverbs 16:18: *"Pride goes before destruction, and a haughty spirit before a fall."* Her act of defiance was fueled by pride, which never wants to submit to authority but always insists on having its own way. Vashti took pride to the palace and lost her position as a result. If we have pride in our hearts (and all of us do), we need to uproot that prideful spirit, or we will be disqualified from the selection process of standard setters in God's kingdom.

You Can't Take Pride to the Palace

Pride is very deceptive, and I can imagine that Vashti thought her position was "in the bag." Pride blinds you into thinking that you're irreplaceable, that nobody else could fill your shoes. In reality, any one of us could lose our position overnight and be replaced by someone with a humble, teachable heart.

Pride is the opposite of humility, a character quality that precipitated Esther's path to the palace. And it prevents us from practicing humility because pride expects to be served rather than seeks to serve. No one deserves to be served except Jesus! What a deception.

The spirit of pride can cause you to be deceived in so many ways. And spiritual pride is the worst, in my opinion, because it keeps a heart from being teachable—a key of humility that we've already discussed. Those with spiritual pride presume to know it all. They think they are hearing from God, and no one can tell them otherwise. It's really a very dangerous place because they are no longer under anyone's authority. Throughout my years of ministry, I have seen people lose their families, their ministries, and almost everything else because of pride. Pride is an ugly, ungodly root that is very destructive.

When you serve your boss, when you serve the men and women of God in your life, you are radically blessed. I have received more blessings from serving than from doing anything else. When you serve, you sow blessings into their lives, and you always reap an impartation of their anointing in your own life. If you serve the devil, you receive an impartation from him. But when you serve God, along with the men and women He has anointed, you receive an impartation into your life from the anointing that's on their lives. Pride, on the other hand, blocks this blessing because it keeps you from serving wholeheartedly.

When we have pride in our hearts, our primary motivation will be to bring honor to ourselves. We'll always be focused on getting ahead and staying ahead.

Get to the Root of the Problem

It's hard to uproot the pride in your heart unless you're aware of its origins. Often, a prideful spirit stems from a sense of insecurity, as people boast and put on airs to conceal their self-doubts. The flesh may employ carnal defense mechanisms, such as self-assertion and boasting, without being aware of it. Prideful people often figure that if they can mask their feelings of inferiority by asserting themselves and lording it over other people, it will protect their egos and emotions. One way they can mask those feelings is by developing a sense of superiority and exaggerated self-worth. Yet this is a temporary fix to get through the situation at hand. If we are to find freedom from the lies of the enemy, we must locate and dig up the root of our pride. The lies of the enemy go something like this: "You aren't worthy." "You're stupid." "Everyone else is better than you." "You will never amount to anything."

As a young evangelist, I was the only woman preacher in my circle of friends and in the churches I visited. That's not to say that I wasn't intimidated by all of the men! To make matters worse, most of those men were old enough to be my father—or even my grandfather. I didn't have gender or age on my side, not to mention the sense of insecurity, which was rooted deeply in childhood.

Pride became my way of dealing with the overwhelming situation I found myself in. I wanted to fulfill the call of God on my life, and I wanted to walk in obedience to the Holy Spirit, but it totally freaked me out to talk in front of people. And it was very intimidating to me that there were no other women (especially women under twenty-one) doing what I was doing.

I had unknowingly employed the defense mechanism of pride. After I had spent a year or two traveling full-time as a minister, the Lord spoke to me. He showed me my pride and told me point-blank that pride was my way of dealing with a sense of insecurity.

The Lord spoke truth to me that day, and I had to choose to allow Him to set me free of my sense of insecurity. It didn't happen overnight. But, through a process of renewing my mind by the Word of truth and choosing to hold on to the rope of hope (God's Word), I was healed and set free. Today, I love speaking the Word of God before people more than anything else in life. I love my call and I consider it a great privilege.

Insecure people never like to be corrected. They perceive correction as rejection, when, in reality, it is not. When we are able to receive correction with gratitude, it means that we have a teachable heart. Pride is often too insecure to admit any shortcomings or limited knowledge of any sort. Let's get real!

God is the only one who is perfect and all-knowing. So, you are going to have to get over it! But be sure to do so in a healthy manner—by renewing your mind with the Word of truth. Your ego no longer needs the protection of pride because you know who you are, and it doesn't depend on other people and your superiority to them.

Pride strives to be perfect. Pride strives to be right at all times. Pride strives to reach the top, no matter the cost or the cutthroat methods involved. Stop striving and start thriving! This happens when you live with a spirit of humility. Pride can cause you to get what I call "stuck on the treadmill." When you get "stuck on the treadmill," you can't get off. You keep striving to achieve. You keep striving to prove yourself to number one—yourself! And you can also get caught up in proving yourself to everyone else. Don't strive for the acceptance of people. Rest in the Lord and seek to have a pure heart. That's what impresses the Lord. Who are you trying to impress today? Yourself? Others? Stop striving and start enjoying everyday life. Striving takes the fun out of living.

If you get "stuck on the treadmill," you'll eventually fall off. That's what happened to Vashti. She fell from her high position and watched as her crown was placed on the head of another. Have you ever fallen off of a treadmill? It really hurts! It injures you, and until you get away from the treadmill that's in motion, you continue to incur personal injury.

The Antidote to Pride

God hates pride. *"To fear the LORD is to hate evil; I hate pride and arrogance, evil behavior and perverse speech"* (Proverbs 8:13). Pride destroys, pride deceives, and pride distorts the truth. It was pride that caused Satan to fall from heaven. (See Isaiah 14.)

Humility, on the other hand, wants to serve and not to be served. It's a picture of our Lord and Savior, Jesus Christ, who *"did not come to be served, but to serve, and to give his life as a ransom for many"* (Matthew 20:28; Mark 10:45).

Humble Yourself before the Lord

The first part of the pride "antidote" is to humble ourselves before the Lord. We must understand that the Lord hates pride and seeks to work His humility in our lives. We can have this humility worked in our lives the easy way or the hard way. The choice is up to us.

First Peter 5:6 says, *"Humble yourselves, therefore, under God's mighty hand, that he may lift you up in due time."* If we obey the Word and humble ourselves, then God doesn't have to do it. And if we don't, He'll still get the job done—we just might not appreciate the methods. If He has to, He will humble us publicly. And the more public your position is, the more public your humbling will be. I advise you to go ahead and humble yourself daily in prayer. It's a lot easier that way, and it hurts a lot less!

> If we obey the Word and humble ourselves, then God doesn't have to do it. And if we don't, He'll still get the job done—we just might not appreciate the methods.

Every day, we have opportunities to humble ourselves. We can do so by putting others first, by actively serving them, and by not thinking more highly of ourselves than we ought. (See Romans 12:3.) We also can humble ourselves by living a lifestyle of prayer and Bible reading, for it's while we're praying and meditating on the Word that the Lord speaks to our hearts concerning their contents. If we remain in God's presence, He will daily lead us in paths of humility.

What does God require of us? The same thing He required of Esther, and the same thing He requires of all standard setters: *"To act justly and to love mercy and to walk humbly with your God"* (Micah 6:8). That's the job description of all palace personnel. We must act in ways that are righteous and just. We must act justly, love mercy, and walk humbly with the Lord. No one can take pride to the palace—God loves us enough not to let us. He doesn't want us to get kicked out, like Vashti did.

Forgive Instead of Fighting

Pride is one of the greatest hindrances to our love walk. It's hard to walk in love toward others when our pride is constantly putting "self" front and center.

I recently prayed and told the Lord that I wanted to increase in my love walk, to take it to a higher level. Soon after I prayed, someone who had been making false accusations against me launched an all-out verbal attack. Talk about an immediate answer to prayer—this was the perfect opportunity for me to practice walking in love instead of giving in to my fleshly instinct to defend myself. A prideful spirit always jumps to its own defense, but love does just the opposite. There is no focus on "self" when we walk and live in love. God wants to be our defense. He wants to defend us. When we try to defend ourselves, it's because we are focused on "self." Where is your focus today? Are you focused on protecting your pride, or are you focused on forgiveness and love?

Jeremiah 50:34 says, *"Yet their Redeemer is strong; the LORD Almighty is his name. He will vigorously defend their cause so that he may bring rest to their land, but unrest to those who live in Babylon."*

The Lord vigorously defends you and your cause. Don't try to defend yourself. We can get in God's way by trying to take matters into our own hands. God is more than capable of taking care of the situation. When you are committed to walking in love and forgiving those who have wounded you, the Lord will give you rest and peace.

> *Because you have made the Lord your refuge, and the Most High your dwelling place, there shall no evil befall you, nor any plague or calamity come near your tent. For He will give His angels [especial] charge over you to accompany and defend and preserve you in all your ways [of obedience and service].* (Psalm 91:9–11 AMP)

When we make the Lord our refuge, when we make the presence of the Lord our dwelling place, we can rest assured that His angels are there to defend us. The Lord sends out back up on our behalf. We even have the angels of the Lord accompanying us and sticking up for us. Who would you rather have defending you—you yourself, or the Lord and all His angels? Let God handle it and just focus on being committed to walking in love!

Chapter 7: The Pride Indicator

Points to Ponder

1. Think about a time when you exhibited sinful pride. Can you identify a particular insecurity you were trying to cover?

2. If the insecurity you identified seems to be a regular concern, search the Scriptures for a few verses that you can stand on to combat that sense of insecurity. For example, if you tend to feel insecure about your worth, remember Luke 12:6–7: *"Are not five sparrows sold for two pennies? Yet not one of them is forgotten by God. Indeed, the very hairs of your head are all numbered. Don't be afraid; you are worth more than many sparrows."*

Meditate on these Scriptures, speak them aloud, and commit them to memory:

Pride goes before destruction, and a haughty spirit before a fall.
(Proverbs 16:18)

Do not think of yourself more highly than you ought, but rather think of yourself with sober judgment, in accordance with the measure of faith God has given you.
(Romans 12:3)

The Son of Man did not come to be served, but to serve, and to give his life as a ransom for many.
(Matthew 20:28; Mark 10:45)

Humble yourselves, therefore, under God's mighty hand, that he may lift you up in due time.
(1 Peter 5:6)

— 8 —

THE OBEDIENCE EXAM

When the turn came for Esther (the girl Mordecai had adopted, the daughter of his uncle Abihail) to go to the king, she asked for nothing other than what Hegai, the king's eunuch who was in charge of the harem, suggested....Now the king was attracted to Esther more than to any of the other women, and she won his favor and approval more than any of the other virgins. So he set a royal crown on her head and made her queen instead of Vashti....But Esther had kept secret her family background and nationality just as Mordecai had told her to do, for she continued to follow Mordecai's instructions as she had done when he was bringing her up. (Esther 2:15, 17, 20)

Esther lived a lifestyle of obedience. She understood the importance of being under authority, and she submitted to every authority figure in her life, starting with her parents. When they died, and her cousin Mordecai assumed the responsibility of raising her, her authority figure changed overnight, yet Esther did not waver in her obedience. She was a standard setter because she knew the importance of submitting to authority.

Esther 2:20 says, *"But Esther had kept secret her family background and nationality just as Mordecai had told her to do, for she continued to follow Mordecai's instructions as she had done when he was bringing her up."*

Esther had an obedient heart. She wasn't obedient only when compelled forcibly or coerced; it was just who she was. It was a character trait that had been worked into her life. Long after she left Mordecai's home and was promoted to queen, Esther respected his authority and heeded his advice. Now, that's a smart woman!

When the King calls, we must answer—that's a step of obedience. If we ignore Him, there's always someone else who won't mind coming when He calls. Esther was called upon twice by her husband, the king, and, both times, she answered obediently—a strong contrast to Vashti, for whom the final straw was a refusal to appear at the king's summons. The first time Esther was called was when all of the candidates for queen were gathered.

> *Let the king appoint commissioners in every province of his realm to bring all these beautiful girls into the harem at the citadel of Susa. Let them be placed under the care of Hegai, the king's eunuch, who is in charge of the women; and let beauty treatments be given to them. Then let the girl who pleases the king be queen instead of Vashti.*   (Esther 2:3–4)

The girl who pleased the king was Esther—an ordinary girl with an obedient, submissive heart. She had obeyed Mordecai while under his roof, and then, at the palace, she obeyed Hegai, who was in charge of the harem, asking for nothing more than what he suggested. (See Esther 2:15.) Esther's obedience and submission to the wise counsel of those over her won her favor.

Your Authority Figure May Change, but Your Obedience Shouldn't

When Esther was orphaned and she went to live with Mordecai, her authority figure changed overnight. The same thing happened years later when she went to live in the palace. But she remained unfailingly obedient.

Like Esther, we have to make the proper adjustments when our authority figure changes. It isn't always easy. Think about the transfer of authority when you get a new boss, when you get married, when you move back home. There are many situations and circumstances in which our authority figure changes overnight.

Many years ago, I was on the staff of a large church. I was under the authority of several different leaders, each of whom had a unique style of leadership. I quickly learned that I needed to find out how each leader expected things to be done and then do them in that way. This "research" taught me a lot. It taught me how to work under all types of leadership styles and collaborate with diverse personalities.

I wasn't a puppet on a string, but I was very submissive. Unless an authority figure asks you to do something illegal or immoral, it's best to do what he wants, the way he wants. It may not be the way you would prefer to do it, but if you aren't the boss, it isn't your decision to make. I guarantee you, the boss has a reason why he wants things done that certain way. Just go with the flow, and you will learn a lot.

Working under a variety of leadership styles was actually some of the best ministry training I have ever received. There was one pastor who had a strong personality and was blunt and to the point. Everyone had a hard time working under him, but I "went with the flow." I ended up learning more from him than from any of the other pastors. I learned that he operated with the highest standard of excellence of all the pastors. Yes, he demanded a lot, but in return, I grew and learned more than ever. He taught me to get out of my comfort zone and come into my potential zone, one step of obedience at a time.

The Steps of Obedience

Esther walked in obedience from the first step on her way to the palace, and her path paved the way for her to save an entire nation. We can never get to the last step if we aren't faithful to take the first step.

Your steps are ordered by the Lord. God has placed the steps in a certain order for a reason. You don't have to understand all the steps; you just have to walk in obedience. When Esther was applying for the position of queen, she had no idea that such a weighty task would be set before her. You may not see how all the steps fit together, but that's where faith comes in!

We read in the Psalms, *"The steps of a [good] man are directed and established by the Lord when He delights in his way [and He busies Himself with his every step]"* (Psalm 37:23 AMP). God directs our steps. I always say that hearing from God is easy; it's obeying His voice that's the challenging part. It's challenging to our flesh, because the steps of the journey He leads us on often serve the purpose of killing carnal desires and developing godly character.

We must hear from God on our every choice and decision. We must be led by the Spirit and we must allow the peace of God to be the umpire that rules. In other words, if we don't have peace, we don't make a move or reach a decision. Everything may line up in the natural. All signs may seem to point in a certain direction, but if we don't have total peace in our spirits, we know that it's unwise to proceed, even if we're standing at the altar, about to say "I do." I always say, "If you have doubt, do without, until you have total peace."

Many people are ready to follow where God leads them, but they get frustrated when they find out that the steps God has established for them do not lead to the destination they had in mind. These people then pick their own direction and expect God to establish them in their preferred position. It doesn't work that way!

One definition of *establish* is "to bring about permanently." When God establishes your position, it's permanent! If you establish a business or a ministry, it may not endure; there's no guarantee of stability. But when God establishes something, it's there for good.

> If you have doubt, do without, until you have total peace.

Psalm 90:17 says, *"May the favor of the Lord our God rest upon us; establish the work of our hands for us—yes, establish the work of our hands."* God is the one who establishes us and establishes the work of our hands. If you are trying to establish yourself or your work, good luck! But when God establishes you, look out! Be prepared for supernatural blessings, opened doors, and favor wherever you go.

Psalm 37:23 (AMP) says that the Lord *"busies Himself"* with your every step. In other words, God makes your every step His business! You don't have to understand why this step or that step is so important. God is the one who connects the dots. When all the dots are not yet connected, you can't see the big picture clearly, if at all. Yet, once the Holy Spirit starts connecting the dots—your every step over the last week, month, year, or decade—the picture becomes increasingly clear! Eventually, you will see the beautiful picture that the Lord has seen all along.

Don't work hard trying to make things happen. Don't work hard trying to open doors to the fulfillment of your vision. Work hard at walking in obedience—even when God gives us instructions that sound illogical to our finite minds. For we will reach our final destination only when we follow obediently in the path laid out for us. When God says to get out of the boat and walk on the water, we need to get out of the boat and walk on the water. When God says to go, we must go, even if we don't understand where we are going.

Abraham didn't have a clue where he was going, but when God said to go, he went without question. And it is because he obeyed God's command that we're here today.

"The LORD *had said to Abram* [as he was called originally], *'Leave your country, your people and your father's household and go to the land I will show you'"* (Genesis 12:1–4). Abraham's first step was that of obedience. Your first step—your every step, really—needs to be a step of obedience. But if your first step is not one of obedience, you will never make it to the last step or fulfill your call and vision.

We should be quick to obey the voice of the Holy Spirit and never "flirt" with detours or side shows. We "flirt" with detours when we have heard God say not to do something or not to go somewhere, but we keep entertaining the thought in our mind, anyhow. We try to talk ourselves into it. We begin to think, *Maybe that wasn't God telling me not to do that. I was probably just imagining it.* Never "flirt" with a detour from God's ordained path for your life. Detours can be very destructive, as they derail you from fulfilling God's purpose for your life.

Don't ever buy the lie from the enemy when he says, "This little bit won't hurt. You can do it just this once, and no one will ever know." Satan comes to steal, kill, and destroy. (See John 10:10.) And he plays for keeps!

Proverbs 28:13 says, *"He who conceals his sins does not prosper, but whoever confesses and renounces them finds mercy."* If you are concealing your sin today and you think no one knows, that's a lie of the enemy. Let me remind you that God knows everything, and His opinion is the only one that counts. The only person who is really being fooled is you, so don't be deceived by the enemy any longer. Get things right with God. Repent of your sin and ask the Holy Spirit to give you the power to stay on course to fulfill God's plan for your life. Then, pray and ask God to give you some Holy-Ghost-filled Christian friends who will encourage you to live an obedient life of holiness and righteousness.

Avoid Getting Detoured by Disobedience

Too bad for Vashti—she wasn't smart. Just because God has blessed us with a position and an anointing doesn't mean that He will keep us in that place no matter what. Our choices, our decisions, and our obedience will determine how long we stay in our God given positions. And, if we choose not to obey, God always has someone waiting to take our place.

Yes, God had called Vashti to a royal position, but with that position came the responsibility to live in such a way as to please the king. Vashti was required to live a lifestyle of obedience and standards. But she refused the responsibility her position entailed. And so, God raised up Esther.

Esther 1:19 says,

"Therefore, if it pleases the king, let him issue a royal decree and let it be written in the laws of Persia and Media, which cannot be repealed, that Vashti is never again to enter the presence of King Xerxes. Also let the king give her royal position to someone else who is better than she."

Our choices can disqualify us from our positions forever! It's not worth losing your job, your family, or your ministry over one impulsive decision. Esau sold his birthright to Jacob for a bowl of stew—how silly! Many people sell their birthright—their anointing and place in God—for a quick satisfaction of the flesh. Esau's fleshly satisfaction lasted only a few moments, just long enough to eat some bread and a bowl of porridge. Then, he got up and left. (See Genesis 25:33–34.) He left with his flesh temporarily satisfied and with his birthright gone forever. Our birthright lasts longer than we do. Our birthright or our call and anointing gets passed on to the next generation. But Esau didn't have a birthright or an anointing to pass on. He had only the temporary satisfaction that comes from eating. At the heart of his birthright were the covenant promises that Isaac had inherited from Abraham. But the promises of God are conditional upon our heart of obedience.

Is it really worth it? Is a temporary, momentary flesh satisfier worth losing your birthright, your anointing, your family, your ministry, or your career? The devil would tell you it is, but you know different. Don't allow anyone who is standing in the wings to replace you from what God has called and anointed you to do.

Of course, nothing can disqualify us eternally from the love of God. If we acknowledge our wrongdoing and repent, God will always love us no matter what. But King Xerxes wasn't God, and so Vashti was never again restored to her position. Instead, the king gave her position to someone *"better than she."* Notice that *"better"* didn't mean "more educated," "more beautiful," or "more successful"—it meant "obedient"!

Disobedience Costs You Your Anointing

While obedience to the Lord imparts His anointing, disobedience puts us at odds with God and costs us the anointing. This is what happened to Saul in 1 Samuel 15. The prophet Samuel had anointed Saul king of Israel and commanded him on behalf of God to *"go, attack the Amalekites and totally destroy everything that belongs to them. Do not spare them; put to death men and women, children and infants, cattle and sheep, camels and donkeys"* (verse 3).

God's instructions to Samuel were to *"totally destroy everything."* In Greek, *everything* means "everything." In Hebrew, *everything* means "everything." When God says "everything," He means *everything!*

> *But Saul and the army spared Agag and the best of the sheep and cattle, the fat calves and lambs—everything that was good. These they were unwilling to destroy completely, but everything that was despised and weak they totally destroyed.* (verse 9)

Now, was that what God had said to do? No! They kept the best for themselves. They kept everything that was good for themselves. The Lord told Saul to destroy everything, but he only destroyed the despised and weak things. Total, immediate obedience is what the Lord requires. We don't get to pick and choose the commands we feel like obeying. God rejected Saul as king because of his disobedience. Partial obedience is really disobedience. And so the Lord was grieved that He had made Saul king.

First Samuel 15:11 says, *"I am grieved that I have made Saul king, because he has turned away from me and has not carried out my instruction...."* Saul did not set a standard of obedience. He failed the obedience test. And, as a result, he lost his position. *"For rebellion is like the sin of divination, and arrogance like the evil of idolatry. Because you have rejected the word of the LORD, he has rejected you as king"* (1 Samuel 15:23).

> Total, immediate obedience is what the Lord requires. We don't get to pick and choose the commands we feel like obeying.

Disobedience is a sin of rebellion, which is often the result of pride. Someone thinks he knows better than God, and he decides to defy His instructions. But he is treading on thin ice. *"Samuel said to [Saul], 'The LORD has torn the kingdom of Israel from you today and has given it to one of your neighbors—to one better than you'"* (1 Samuel 15:28).

If you and I choose not to walk in obedience, the Lord always has someone with a heart of obedience who would be honored to take our place. We must not grieve the Lord with our choices. I never want the Lord to be sorry that He put me in a place or in a certain position. As we stay close to the Lord through prayer, through the study of His Word, and through fellowship with the Holy Spirit, we can maintain a walk of obedience and fulfill our assignment for the king.

Doubt Invites Disobedience

Disobedience will disqualify you from a high position or place in God quicker than anything else. The first example was when man first sinned, in the garden of Eden, and was kicked out forever. The consequences of Adam and Eve's disobedience have endured through the ages, condemning all of us to eternal death unless we call on the Lord as our Savior.

In Genesis 2:16–17, it says, *"And the* Lord *God commanded the man, 'You are free to eat from any tree in the garden; but you must not eat from the tree of the knowledge of good and evil, for when you eat of it you will surely die.'"*

God's instructions were plain and simple. He wasn't denying Adam food from any of the other trees, but He made it very clear that Adam was not to eat from the tree of the knowledge of good and evil.

So, what did Adam do? He ate from the tree of the knowledge of good and evil—not smart! Disobedience is never smart. It always costs more than you can pay and takes you further than you ever wanted to go in the wrong direction.

Doubt is an enemy of obedience. If the devil can get you to doubt the voice of the Lord, if he can get you to doubt what God said, his chances of getting you to fall into disobedience are greater. Doubt was the tactic Satan used to entice Adam and Eve to sin. Genesis 3:1 says, *"Now the serpent was more crafty than any of the wild animals the* Lord *God had made. He said to the woman, 'Did God really say, "You must not eat from any tree in the garden"?'"*

The enemy doesn't have any new tricks. God is the Creator; the devil is just the imitator. The devil never creates new tricks; he just tries to catch you off guard with the old ones. We fail to realize how many times the enemy tries to trip us up by calling into question the commands of God and whispering to us, "Did God really say such and such?"

As we seek to obey God, one of the things we need the most is discernment, for this is how we can negate the devil's sly arguments. We must also dwell in the presence of God and immerse ourselves in His Word, through which He speaks to us, so that we will be able to hear His voice (and discern it as such). Joshua 1:8 says, *"Do not let this Book of the Law depart from your mouth; meditate on it day and night, so that you may be careful to do everything written in it. Then you will be prosperous and successful."* When we are careful to obey the Word of God, we will be prosperous and successful. We must be careful to do everything the Lord tells us to do. We can't pick and choose. We can't obey the "second opinions" in our lives. We must obey completely and immediately if we want to be prosperous and successful. Then, and only then, will things go well for us. After all, that's the whole point. The Lord wants us to have the best, and when we follow His instructions, that's exactly what we receive—His best for our lives! Then, when Satan asks you, "Did God really say such and such?" you can give him a definitive "Yes!"

Disobedience Takes You Down, but You Don't Have to Stay There

Jonah was an intelligent man who had a dumb moment. Have you ever had a dumb moment, better known as a stupid choice? I think we all have. Jonah intended to escape his divinely appointed task. Let me just clue you in—that never works! We can't run from God. Well, I suppose we can, but we won't get very far, and we'll wish we never had!

This sense of regret was certainly Jonah's experience. The book about his epic adventure begins,

> *The word of the LORD came to Jonah son of Amittai: "Go to the great city of Nineveh and preach against it, because its wickedness has come up before me." But Jonah ran away from the LORD and headed for Tarshish. He went down to Joppa, where he found a ship bound for that port. After paying the fare, he went aboard and sailed for Tarshish to flee from the LORD.* (Jonah 1:1–3)

Jonah heard a word from the Lord. He received his instructions. But he decided not to heed them. Let me give you some advice—*always* do what the Lord tells you to do, so that it will go well with you. I mean, it's brainless, really, yet we disobey the Lord all too often.

Now, stop and think for a minute. Do you really think you can run away from God? You are smarter than that—but, obviously, Jonah wasn't.

> Let me give you some advice—*always* do what the Lord tells you to do, so that it will go well with you.

The Word says that Jonah *"went **down** to Joppa."* Disobedience will always drag you down a path that takes you further away from the Lord. After Jonah went down to Joppa, sure enough, he found a ship going in the direction he wanted to go. I bet he thought, *Well, that's my confirmation! I knew God wouldn't mind.* I bet he even began to doubt if God had really told him to go to Nineveh, after all. When we ignore the Lord's instructions, we often come up with ways to justify our disobedience. We talk ourselves into believing that everything is all right. We doubt the Word of God and heed the devil instead because we're really hoping that we misheard God, that He didn't really say what we think He said.

Several years ago, when I was a pastor on staff at a large church, a young man from the congregation came by my office to ask me if I thought it was God's will for him to marry the young lady he had been dating. I told him that he would have to pray and hear from God for himself and just do whatever the Lord told him to do. A few weeks passed, and he stopped by my office again to ask me the same question. I gave him the same answer.

This went on for months and months. During one of his visits, the Lord told me that this young man already knew it wasn't God's will for him to marry the girl in question. God said, "He didn't like My answer, so he's coming by your office to get a second opinion!"

How many times do we try to get a "second opinion" for a question that the Lord has already answered? Jonah didn't even ask for a second opinion; he just ran with his own opinion and paid a fare that seemed cheap at the time. The fare to disobedience is never "cheap"—it only seems like it is at the time.

Disobedience can end up costing you everything, as it did Vashti. It was only by the grace of God that disobedience didn't cost Jonah his life. Disobedience can cost you the ultimate price—your life and even your salvation—if you are not careful.

Obedience brings blessings, but disobedience brings storms. Jonah 1:4 says, *"Then the LORD sent a great wind on the sea, and such a violent storm arose that the ship threatened to break up."* The Lord sent a storm in order to get Jonah back on the path He had ordained for him. Sometimes, you find yourself in a situation where your ship—or your life—is threatening to break into a million pieces because your heavenly Father is trying to get you back on track.

Jonah still had a choice to make, and this time, he made the right one. He chose to obey God's commands. Jonah 1:12 records what he said to the crew and his fellow passengers on the storm-tossed ship: *"Pick me up and throw me into the sea…and it will become calm. I know that this is my fault that this great storm has come upon you."*

In other words, Jonah was saying, "I know that I've disobeyed." He owned the responsibility for the storm. He didn't shift the blame. He didn't search for a scapegoat. He acknowledged his mistake.

That confession was all that God needed to hear. After Jonah was thrown overboard, *"The LORD provided a great fish to swallow Jonah, and Jonah was inside the fish three days and three nights"* (Jonah 1:17). The Lord made provision for Jonah when he acknowledged his sin of disobedience. And He will miraculously provide for us when we choose to walk in obedience. No matter what your mess is today, and no matter what you did to land there, make the choice to get up out of your mess by obeying the Lord. Your heavenly Father will hold your hand and gently lead you out one step at a time and put you back on the path of obedience.

Chapter 8: The Obedience Exam

Points to Ponder

1. Who do you consider to be the primary authority in your life? (God? Your boss? A parent? Your spouse?) To what degree do you find it easy to submit to that authority?

2. Which particular area(s) of your life do you find it particularly difficult to submit to a corresponding authority figure? Why do you think that is?

3. The Bible says that the Lord orders the steps of a good man (see Psalm 37:23 AMP) and that He maps out a positive future for those who love Him (see Jeremiah 29:11). How can an understanding of these Scriptures help you to submit to His will and obey His directives?

4. Have you ever "flirted" with a detour from the will of God? What were the consequences?

5 What is the relationship between doubt and disobedience? How does this correlation play out in your life?

Meditate on these Scriptures, speak them aloud, and commit them to memory:

Do not let this Book of the Law depart from your mouth; meditate on it day and night, so that you may be careful to do everything written in it. Then you will be prosperous and successful. (Joshua 1:8)

He who conceals his sins does not prosper, but whoever confesses and renounces them finds mercy. (Proverbs 28:13)

The authorities that exist have been established by God. Consequently, he who rebels against the authority is rebelling against what God has instituted, and those who do so will bring judgment on themselves. (Romans 13:1–2)

Obey your leaders and submit to their authority. They keep watch over you as men who must give an account. Obey them so that their work will be a joy, not a burden, for that would be of no advantage to you. (Hebrews 13:17)

— 9 —

THE TEST OF INTEGRITY

Then Esther sent this reply to Mordecai: "Go, gather together all the Jews who are in Susa, and fast for me. Do not eat or drink for three days, night or day. I and my maids will fast as you do. When this is done, I will go to the king, even though it is against the law. And if I perish, I perish."... Queen Esther answered [the king], "If I have found favor with you, O king, and if it pleases your majesty, grant me my life—this is my petition. And spare my people—this is my request. For I and my people have been sold for destruction and slaughter and annihilation. If we had merely been sold as male and female slaves, I would have kept quiet, because no such distress would justify disturbing the king." King Xerxes asked Queen Esther, "Who is he? Where is the man who has dared to do such a thing?" Esther said, "The adversary and enemy is this vile Haman."

(Esther 4:15–16; 7:3–6)

Esther's integrity protected her in her pursuit of the palace, and her integrity protected her as a shield once she arrived there, so that the fate of Vashti would not befall her. Psalm 25:21 says, *"May integrity and uprightness protect me, because my hope is in you."* Our uprightness and our integrity propel us into high positions and then protect us while we're there. We can put our hope in the fact that when we act with integrity, the Lord always protects us every step of the way. Integrity will uphold us in all that we do.

The king knew Esther's heart. Her integrity of heart protected her when she uncovered the conspiracy to kill the Jews. She risked her life by going before the king without having been summoned and by revealing her identity as a Jew, one of the very people Haman's plot was hatched to kill. Our integrity of heart protects us, as well.

Integrity is defined as "adherence to moral and ethical principles; soundness of moral character; honesty; the state of being whole, entire, or undiminished." That's a complex definition, but it's appropriate, since integrity has many facets. Just when you thought this was a single test—surprise! The integrity test has several components that you need to pass on your way to the palace.

First, though, let's look at an excellent description of integrity from the Psalms. Psalm 15 could easily serve as an answer key when the Test Administrator is grading us on integrity.

> *Who may dwell in your sanctuary? Who may live on your holy hill? He whose walk is blameless and who does what is righteous, who speaks the truth from his heart and has no slander on his tongue, who does his neighbor no wrong and casts no slur on his fellowman, who despises a vile man but honors those who fear the LORD, who keeps his oath even when it hurts, who lends his money without usury and does not accept a bribe against the innocent. He who does these things will never be shaken.* (Psalm 15:1–5)

Pass the Test and Be Blessed

Yes, God tests our hearts in order to build integrity in each of us. Father God wants each of us to have a heart of integrity. We develop that heart as we pass the Father's tests.

First Chronicles 29:17 says, *"I know, my God, that you test the heart and are pleased with integrity."* Our heavenly Father is pleased with integrity. It is of utmost importance to the Lord. He was pleased with Esther's integrity, and her integrity placed her in the palace. As standard setters, we must have the integrity of the Father in order to approach our palace and position in the Lord.

We have to pass the integrity test. And it's a test we must pass continually. We may even be faced with a pop quiz from time to time. Just because we passed the attitude test with flying colors a few days ago doesn't mean that we will never have to pass that test again.

God loves us so much that He patiently administers a battery of tests that are strategically designed to qualify us for the integrity of a standard setter in these last days. Will you obey the voice of the Holy Spirit and do the honest thing? Integrity would say yes and cause you to pass the test.

The Test of Faithfulness and Loyalty

When we have integrity toward other people, we are faithful and loyal. Faithful people are people you can trust, people who have proven themselves reliable. Esther was faithful and loyal to Mordecai and to King Xerxes, and especially to her people when they needed her the most.

Esther's kind of faithfulness is hard to find. As it says in Proverbs 20:6, *"Many a man claims to have unfailing love, but a faithful man who can find?"* Yes, faithful people are hard to find. But standard setters are faithful because they have allowed the testing of the Lord to work integrity in them! When you pass the faithfulness test and the loyalty test, you will be both blessed and protected by the hand of God.

Psalm 37:28–29 says, *"For the LORD loves the just and will not forsake his faithful ones. They will be protected forever, but the offspring of the wicked will be cut off; the righteous will inherit the land and dwell in it forever."* The Lord never forsakes His faithful children. Even when we fail the faithfulness test, the Lord lovingly reschedules us for another test taking time.

A rare form of loyalty was exhibited in the character of Ruth. She was faithful to her mother-in-law, Naomi, and determined to stay with her, even when Naomi urged her to go back to her people, where she could find a new husband. Ruth refused, saying,

> *Don't urge me to leave you or to turn back from you. Where you go I will go, and where you stay I will stay. Your people will be my people and your God my God. Where you die I will die, and there I will be buried. May the LORD deal with me, be it ever so severely, if anything but death separates you and me.* (Ruth 1:16–17)

Ruth's character and integrity made her fiercely loyal to Naomi. They kept her in position, though she had plenty of opportunities to turn around and run after her own interests. And her faithfulness opened the door to her miracle, for it caused her to cross paths with Boaz, her eventual kinsman-redeemer and husband.

Loyalty is a decision, and it doesn't always come easy. What is your decision today? Will you be faithful, like Ruth, and loyal to the end? If so, you, too, will be blessed beyond measure and lifted to the position of a standard setter.

The Test of Righteousness

Righteousness is simply doing the right thing. If we listen to the Lord's voice and obey His instructions, we will be able to say with David, that the Lord *"leads me in the paths of righteousness for His name's sake"* (Psalm 23:3 NKJV).

God gave us the following instruction, for example, through the pen of the apostle Paul:

Do not offer the parts of your body to sin, as instruments of wickedness, but rather offer yourselves to God, as those who have been brought from death to life; and offer the parts of your body to him as instruments of righteousness. (Romans 6:13)

When we accept Christ into our lives and offer ourselves to Him, sin is no longer our master. We are no longer slaves to sin. Instead, we become God's *"instruments of righteousness."*

Paul went on to say,

Don't you know that when you offer yourselves to someone to obey him as slaves, you are slaves to the one whom you obey—whether you are slaves to sin, which leads to death, or to obedience, which leads to righteousness? (Romans 6:16)

Obedience to the leading of the Holy Spirit will cultivate the fruit of righteousness in your character. When you have the righteousness of Christ, the Holy Spirit will nudge you and show you how to act, speak, and respond in every situation, so that you may set a standard of righteousness with your life.

Here is the next part of Paul's argument:

Just as you used to offer the parts of your body in slavery to impurity and to ever-increasing wickedness, so now offer them in slavery to righteousness leading to holiness. (Romans 6:19)

Righteousness reflects your relationship with the Lord and affects your relationships with other people. And it all starts with obedience. When you walk in obedience, righteousness will mark your relationships, and you will be headed in the direction of a holy life. You can't qualify as holy unless you treat others in a righteous way, as opposed to a self-righteous way.

Again, when we live a righteous life, we do the "right" thing in response to God's Word and in our relationships with other people.

Recently, a member of my staff scheduled a guest minister for an event, but, due to miscommunication, there was a scheduling conflict that resulted in our having to cancel his visit. It was not completely clear where the fault lay—whether the error was committed by my staff member or his ministry—but the Lord told me to do the righteous thing. Even though we cancelled the speaker, the Lord said, "I want you to do the righteous thing. I want you to send him his honorarium anyway."

Obediently, I went to the accounting department to have them make out a check to him. At this point, the Lord said, "I want you to give him double for his trouble." So, what did I do next? You guessed it! I wrote him out a check for double the amount that we had committed to give him, even though he never came to minister.

It always pays to do the righteous thing. When we pursue other, sinful paths and stray from the presence of the Lord, we miss out on His direction and blessings for our lives. But, when we lead righteous lives, we are filled with the power and the glory of God as we dwell continually in His presence.

The Test of Speech

One of the hardest tests for most of us to pass is what I like to call the "mouth test." It's the words of our mouths that show what is in our hearts and indicate whether we have integrity.

We have the following instructions in Ephesians 4:29–30:

Do not let any unwholesome talk come out of your mouths, but only what is helpful for building others up according to their needs, that it may benefit those who listen. And do not grieve the Holy Spirit of God, with whom you were sealed for the day of redemption.

We are not supposed to "let" unwholesome talk come out of our mouths. Our mouths are supposed to be sharpened swords for the glory of God. We are to use our words to build up the kingdom of God and to edify His people.

And we are to tear down the kingdom of darkness by speaking and praying the Word of God.

Your mouth says a lot about you! You may not be talking about yourself, but the words of your mouth reveal the condition of your heart and the depth of your integrity. Let's pray every day, *"May the words of my mouth and the meditation of my heart be pleasing in your sight, O Lord, my Rock and my Redeemer"* (Psalm 19:14).

In our daily life, we use air filters and water filters, but I believe we need to have a "life filter" to purify our hearts, our attitudes, our thoughts, our actions, and especially our words. Our "life filter" is the Word of God, and it's operated by the power of the Holy Spirit. We can develop a life filter that purifies our thoughts and our words when we meditate on the Word of God.

Believers say all kinds of things that should never make it past their life filter. They think, speak, and act without first passing those things through their life filter. But standard setters have their life filters in full operation every day.

When we "let" impurities pass through our life filter and speak words we shouldn't, we grieve the Holy Spirit. Are you only saying things that build other people up and benefit the one who is listening to you talk? If not, you'd better adjust your filter! In the presence of the Lord, we can get our daily adjustments as needed.

The Test of Sound Stewardship

Any test that involves money is a difficult one, but your favor will grow by leaps and bounds once you have passed this test. The money test shows where your heart really is.

At Joy Ministries, I have a hardworking staff. Most, if not all, of them would probably continue to work for Joy Ministries, even if I could not afford to give them a paycheck. Most of them would work another job to pay their bills and volunteer their time to do the ministry. They consider it an honor to be in the ministry, and if they had to pay their bills by another means and work for free they would—all because they love God and His work. They have all passed the money test.

If you haven't passed the money test and you are in the ministry, you may be lacking in a critical area of your integrity. No one should be in the ministry as means of earning. Yes, the workman is worthy of his hire (see Luke 10:7), but if you wouldn't be willing to do your ministry without pay, there is something missing in your heart.

A pastor once told me that he could think of no other job where he could make as much money as he did at his church. I was shocked at his comment! I worked at Joy Ministries without compensation for many years because I put everything I made back into the ministry.

I'm not saying God wants to keep His ministers poor. I believe just the opposite. And that's why it's so important to pass the money test. If you don't pass the money test, God can't put all the money in your hand that He wants to. If you haven't passed the money test, God can't get the money out of your hand once He's put it in your hand. You have what I call "sticky hands." All the money God puts in your hand for kingdom purposes get "stuck" to your hand and can't find a way out into the work of the Lord's kingdom.

The key to great blessing is great sowing. However, your heart motive in giving can't be so you will get. Yes, you should expect a harvest—I'm not saying that. But God knows your heart motive, and until your heart motive is right, you won't pass the money test.

Once you pass the money test, you will be blessed beyond measure. God will supernaturally bless you and give you more blessings than you could ever dream. But, He doesn't release all of His blessings until He knows you have the integrity to handle it properly.

The Test of Honesty

Proverbs 10:9 says, *"The man of integrity walks securely, but he who takes crooked paths will be found out."* I have always taught my daughter to be honest no matter what. I would much rather her be honest and tell me something that I don't want to hear than for her to tell me a falsehood that sounds good.

It always pays to be honest. It never pays to be dishonest. Don't allow the enemy to tell you it's easier to just tell a "little white lie." First of all, there are no "little white lies." A lie is a lie, and the truth is the truth. The truth will always be made known, so just go ahead and be honest the first time around!

The devil is a liar and the father of all lies. (See John 8:44.) Don't ever act like the devil by lying, and never give him an open door through your choice to be deceptive. You have heard it said, "Honesty is the best policy." Well, honesty is the only policy in my house, and the same is true in the kingdom of God. Always be honest. Integrity is always honest. The walk of integrity is always a safe one because there's no fear of slipping up and telling the wrong story.

The Test of Leadership

A true test of integrity is to be placed in a position of leadership, for it's there that you're on display. Your authority is protected only as long as you are leading with integrity. Otherwise, you may be impeached, as happens to U.S. presidents when their lack of integrity is exposed. When you lead without integrity, God can remove you overnight from the place He put you in.

Psalm 78:72 says, *"And David shepherded them with integrity of heart; with skillful hands he led them."* The Lord is looking for leaders who will lead His people as a shepherd leads his sheep.

Integrity of heart qualifies you for the position. Would you like to be in full-time ministry today? Would you like to be promoted on your job to a position much higher than the one you are in today? Well, if you lead with integrity of heart, God will open the door and put you in the palace at His appointed time. He did it for Esther, and He will do it for you!

> The walk of integrity is always a safe one because there's no fear of slipping up and telling the wrong story.

Job Scored 100 Percent on the Integrity Test

Perhaps the best example of someone who passed the integrity test was Job. And he did so through trial by fire! He endured some of our greatest fears—the loss of family, possessions, and health—but he never once compromised his integrity.

> *Then the LORD said to Satan, "Have you considered my servant Job? There is no one on earth like him; he is blameless and upright, a man who fears God and shuns evil. And he still maintains his integrity, though you incited me against him to ruin him without any reason."* (Job 2:3)

Job remained loyal to God, never blaming Him for his situations. Do you curse God and throw away your standard of integrity when tough times stare you in the face? Or do you maintain your integrity no matter what? Maybe you do a good job until someone tries to influence you in a negative way. Poor Job. His wife said to him, *"Are you still holding on to your integrity? Curse God and die!"* (Job 2:9).

What an encouraging wife, right? But Job refused to turn his back on God. He determined to keep holding on and set a standard of faith, even in the midst of unimaginable trials. In response to his wife, Job replied, *"You are talking like a foolish woman. Shall we accept good from God, and not trouble?"* (Job 2:10). That verse concludes with this statement: *"In all this, Job did not sin in what he did."* In all this—all the trials, all the hardships, all the losses, all the difficult times—Job did not sin in his heart attitude, his thoughts, or his words. Wow. That's integrity!

On top of that, when Job's so-called friends did nothing but heap blame and discouragement upon him, Job *"prayed for his friends,"* and then *"the LORD made him prosperous again and gave him twice as much as he had before"* (Job 42:10). Job's prayer marked the turning point for him. Because he forgave, because he kept his heart right with God and man, God was able to bless him with greater abundance than before.

Learning to live a lifestyle of forgiveness is vital as we grow in integrity. The Word says that if we don't forgive others that hurt and offend us, God the Father can't forgive us. (See Matthew 6:15.) We can't put on our "church face" and have unforgiveness in our hearts. We must forgive no matter what the offense has been. Unforgiveness is like a cancer that slowly eats away and eventually kills a person spiritually, emotionally, and possibly even physically.

When the world is against you, and the people around you wonder why you still have faith, try saying this out loud: "I'm still holding on! I'm still holding on to Jesus, and I'm still holding on to my integrity, because I'm a standard setter!"

> I would rather be counted among the crazy standard setters than to join the trendsetters any day.

They might think you're crazy, but join the club! I would rather be counted among the crazy standard setters than to join the trendsetters any day. Remember, standard setters hold on to their integrity and stand their ground in the midst of life's storms, while trendsetters (as well as trend followers) who "go with the flow" end up getting carried downstream, far away from their dreams.

Job came out on top. When he reached the other side of his trials with his integrity still intact, he was in an enviable position. He stepped into a double-portion blessing! God gave him double for his trouble. Don't throw away your integrity; it's a pass to the palace—your place of double-portion blessings!

Integrity That Endures

God was building integrity in the life of Esther long before she reached the palace. When God does His work in us, He forms us and builds in our lives in a way that causes them to last eternally. Father wants all of us to be kingdom builders. He builds his character and integrity in us so we in turn will build His kingdom. Esther was just that—a kingdom builder with character and integrity that lasted to the very end.

Psalm 127:1 says, *"Unless the Lord builds the house, its builders labor in vain...."* When we labor to build our will and our desires, we are wasting our time. But when the Lord builds the house—when our heavenly Father builds His character into our lives—we are built to last through any and every situation.

Integrity is a part of any foundation that is built to last. We will never last long without integrity. Vashti didn't last long because she lacked integrity. Esther, on the other hand, had sound moral principles that caused her to last through every trying time. Esther had integrity of heart.

The Lord spoke to Solomon and told him that if he maintained his integrity, as his father David had, his royal throne over Israel would be established forever.

> *When Solomon had finished building the temple of the Lord and the royal palace, and had achieved all he had desired to do, the Lord appeared to him a second time, as he had appeared to him at Gibeon. The Lord said to him: "I have heard the prayer and plea you have made before me; I have consecrated this temple, which you have built, by putting my Name there forever. My eyes and my heart will always be there. As for you, if you walk before me in **integrity of heart** and uprightness, as David your father did, and do all I command and observe my decrees and laws, I will establish your royal throne over Israel forever, as I promised David your father when I said, 'You shall never fail to have a man on the throne of Israel.'"* (1 Kings 9:1–5, emphasis added)

When we have integrity of heart, we are built to last. The guarantee was for Esther, for Solomon, and for you and me today. God told Solomon that what he had built was built to last. God said His name was going to be on the temple forever. And then the Lord said, *"As for you...."* When the Lord spoke to Solomon about him and not the temple building, He was saying, "It's up to you." If Solomon maintained a heart of integrity (like his father David), he, too, would be built to last. But, if Solomon lost his integrity, he would not be assured a lasting future on the royal throne.

The Word records that after Solomon had achieved all he had desired to do, he still had to pass the integrity test. It's so sad when someone achieves everything he had desired, only to lose all of his achievements because of a lack of integrity. We see this played out today in all arenas of life. In order for us to have a solid foundation, in order for us to be standard setters, we must have integrity of heart that lasts. We can't be walking in integrity one day and then walking without integrity the next. If we make bad choices, if we choose not to walk in integrity, we can't expect to be built to last.

> *But if you or your sons turn away from me and do not observe the commands and decrees I have given you and go off to serve other gods and worship them, then I will cut off Israel from the land I have given them and will reject this temple I have consecrated for my Name. Israel will then become a byword and an object of ridicule among all peoples.*   (1 Kings 9:6)

God desires to make us and the work of our hands built to last. But the choice is always up to us. When we choose integrity, we are built to last. When we walk away from our integrity, we are walking away from our solid foundation. Without a solid foundation, nothing can stand.

How sad it is to even think that Israel would have become a *"byword."* In spite of all your achievements, you and all that you have accomplished could become a "byword" if you walk away from your integrity. Without solid integrity of heart, you and I can't stand. Everything will come crashing down around us if we walk away and do not stand in our integrity of heart.

When we maintain integrity in our hearts, we qualify for the top positions in the kingdom of God. Esther qualified for a top position due to her character. The king was looking for a queen who had integrity. Today, the King of Kings is looking for standard setters who have integrity of heart. Those are the ones He will place in high positions. You can never qualify as a standard setter if you don't have integrity of heart.

Psalm 41:12 says, *"In my integrity you uphold me and set me in your presence forever."* Our heart of integrity assures us that God will uphold us in His hand. Integrity is a place of protection for all who will hang on to, not give up, their heart of integrity.

Peace: A True Indication of Integrity

As you allow your integrity to guide you in every choice and decision, you will be successful in all you do. The Word tells us that *"the integrity of the upright guides them"* (Proverbs 11:3). The integrity of the standard setter is what God intended for them to be guided by. The Holy Spirit leads us and guides us. (See John 16:13.) Our standard of integrity sets a framework by which we are to operate daily.

When we are led by integrity, we have peace. When we don't do the right thing or the righteous thing, we lose our peace. Esther had peace in the palace. She wasn't all worried and stressed out about going before the king. She had a standard of integrity that gave her peace in the palace.

What fun is it to go to the palace and not have peace? You can't enjoy anything without peace. What a shame it would be to get to your palace or position in God's purpose for your life and not have peace. Life is too short not to have it!

The lack of peace means there is the presence of stress and worry. The absence of peace means there is the presence of anxiety and fear. God wants to give us supernatural peace in every palace position we find ourselves in. We have confidence when we walk with integrity. That confidence alone brings peace. When we are in right relationship with the Lord, we can have peace within ourselves and in our relationships with others.

Everyone around you doesn't have to like you in order for you to have peace. Everything shouldn't have to be perfect before you can have peace. True peace comes from knowing God and knowing that you are in right relationship with Him. When you are in right relationship with the Lord, you walk with integrity of heart and experience peace.

Esther rested in peace because she had integrity of heart. She was trustworthy, and so the king listened to her plea instead of ending her life, along with the rest of the Jews' lives. Only a heart of integrity could have persuaded the king to take up her cause! The peace with which she approached a proposition that put her life on the line came as a direct result of her integrity of heart.

When you know you have done the right thing, you can have peace as you trust God with the outcome. Enjoy the peace that comes when you've passed the test of integrity!

Chapter 9: The Test of Integrity

Points to Ponder

1. Ruth exhibited rare, unconditional faithfulness toward her mother-in-law, Naomi. Have you ever experienced extraordinary loyalty from a friend or family member? How did it make you feel? Why do you think God values these traits in His children?

2. Are you a "slave" to sin or to righteousness? What steps can you take to move yourself more and more into the camp of slaves of righteousness?

3. Pay attention to the words you speak today. How would your "life filter" score on a scale of 1 to 10, 1 being the most permissive, 10 being the most selective?

4. Job was the victim of some of the worst hardships imaginable, yet he refused to question or curse God, as his wife and "friends" would have had him do. Have you ever questioned God in the midst of difficult circumstances? How can the example of Job help you to react differently in future times of testing?

Meditate on these Scriptures, speak them aloud, and commit them to memory:

May the words of my mouth and the meditation of my heart be pleasing in your sight, O LORD, my Rock and my Redeemer.   (Psalm 19:14)

May integrity and uprightness protect me, because my hope is in you.
(Psalm 25:21)

For the LORD loves the just and will not forsake his faithful ones. They will be protected forever.   (Psalm 37:28)

The integrity of the upright guides them, but the unfaithful are destroyed by their duplicity.   (Proverbs 11:3)

— 10 —

THE BEAUTY CONTEST

Before a girl's turn came to go in to King Xerxes, she had to complete twelve months of beauty treatments prescribed for the women, six months with oil of myrrh and six with perfumes and cosmetics. And this is how she would go to the king: Anything she wanted was given her to take with her from the harem to the king's palace....Now the king was attracted to Esther more than to any of the other women, and she won his favor and approval more than any of the other virgins. So he set a royal crown on her head and made her queen instead of Vashti. (Esther 2:12–13, 17)

Before they could be presented to the king, Esther and the other candidates for queen had to undergo a veritable beauty boot camp that lasted for months. I'm not sure I could handle all of that pampering! Our path to the palace involves a beautification process, but it differs from that of Esther in that we undergo our beauty treatments in the presence of the King rather than before we go to meet Him. We become beautiful and radiant in the Lord's eyes as the result of spending time in His holy presence, for spiritual beauty exceeds every other kind.

Obedience Makes You Attractive

Esther was physically attractive, of course, but the Bible doesn't say that King Xerxes was *"attracted to Esther more than to any of the other women"* because of her good looks. It says that she *"won his favor and approval"* more than any of the others. We've already discussed Esther's favor, which came as the result of her obedience. But the truth is that obedience makes us attractive! The presence of the Lord within Esther made her attractive, just as it is within you.

Spiritual beauty attracts the King. Beauty on the inside—or in our spirits—causes us to be beautiful on the outside. There's nothing more beautiful than a face that radiates the glow that comes from spending time in the Lord's glorious presence! When Moses came down from Mount Sinai with the Ten Commandments, having just spent time with God, his face was so radiant that the Israelites had to shield their eyes from the brightness! (See Exodus 34:29–30.)

In 2010, I was asked to give a testimony on stage with Joyce Meyer at a conference she held in North Carolina. During the day, I fasted and prayed in my hotel room and sought the Lord as to what He wanted me to share that night at the conference. Whenever I'm speaking, whether I'm preaching the entire service or I'm just sharing for a few minutes, I always like to spend quality time with the Lord in preparation. I know that if I spend time in His presence, I will have the glory of the Lord upon me. Then and only then will I have the Word of the Lord. If it's just me speaking, we better all stay home. But, when it's a Word from God, the glory of God falls and the people are radically blessed.

When it was time to leave the hotel for the conference, I could feel the glory of the Lord upon me. As I walked on the platform that night, never having met Joyce Meyer in person before, she literally took a step back and said, "Wow, you are beautiful." God told me it was the glory of God that she saw upon my face. The glory of God makes all of us beautiful!

As we are faithful to get into the presence of the Lord, as we are faithful to live a holy life, the glory of God shines upon us, and the world sees God's beauty all over us. When you choose to spend time in the Lord's presence, the anointing on your life increases. Your greatest asset is your anointing. It's not your education. A lack of education won't keep you from fulfilling God's purpose, but a lack of the anointing could. And that anointing can only come by choosing to spend time in His presence.

Acts 4:13 says, *"When they saw the courage of Peter and John and realized that they were unschooled, ordinary men, they were astonished and they took note that these men had been with Jesus."*

When you have been with the Lord, the glory of God radiates from you. When you are in the presence of the Lord, the Holy Spirit will teach you all things. Peter and John were ordinary men who chose to have a passion for Jesus. As a result, they did astonishing things for the kingdom of God!

Abide in the Vine

We should really be immersed in God's presence 24/7—to "abide in the vine." For that is how we can maintain pure hearts of obedience that attract the Father and His favor, hearts that make us attractive to Him and to other people. But it's important to spend intentional time with God, one-on-one.

Jesus said,

I am the true vine, and my Father is the gardener. He cuts off every branch in me that bears no fruit, while every branch that does bear fruit he prunes so that it will be even more fruitful. You are already clean because of the word I have spoken to you. Remain in me, and I will remain in you. No branch can bear fruit by itself; it must remain in the vine. Neither can you bear fruit unless you remain in me. (John 15:1–4)

Your time of abiding daily in the Lord will change slightly according to the season you are in. When I was traveling with my book tour, I abided in the Lord daily. However, I wasn't able to be home in my prayer room for three hours a day. When my daughter was an infant, I would abide in the vine during her naptimes. The important thing is abiding in the vine daily. As you remain and reside in the presence of the Lord, you will bear beautiful fruit for the kingdom of God.

Vine Abiders Hear the Voice of God

As we dwell in the presence of the Lord by being obedient to Him, we have the ability to hear His voice and discern His guidance. His voice always leads us on a path of righteousness.

Don't allow yourself to be distracted in the pursuit of other paths. There's no better place to be than in the presence of God! In His presence, you can hear clear direction from Him. In His presence, you get the privilege of God's perspective. Everything becomes clear. In His presence, you are reminded of His promises and reassured that He keeps them. In His presence, you see yourself and your circumstances the way God sees them.

When we are distracted from His presence, we often start to push to make things happen instead of pressing into the presence of God and waiting on Him to make things happen. The key is to remain in His presence.

The danger of distraction is obvious in the biblical account of Jesus' visit at the home of Martha and Mary. As you probably know, Martha decided to busy herself with the housework, and it irritated her to no end that, instead of helping, her sister Mary just sat at the feet of Jesus.

> *But Martha was distracted by all the preparations that had to be made. She came to [Jesus] and asked, "Lord, don't you care that my sister has left me to do the work by myself? Tell her to help me!" "Martha, Martha," the Lord answered, "you are worried and upset about many things, but only one thing is needed. Mary has chosen what is better, and it will not be taken away from her."* (Luke 10:40–42)

When you leave your place at Jesus' feet to run after various distractions, your perspective is thrown off balance. You may even become frustrated with fellow believers who "aren't working" but are spending time in prayer, instead. Mary had chosen what was better—the presence of the Lord—and Martha became stressed out and angry as a result, and all because she was *"distracted."* When you fall for distractions and wander from the presence of the Lord, you may be tempted to think that everyone else should be doing what you are doing. But the opposite is true. You should get on your face before the Lord and surrender to Him whatever it is that you've been fretting over.

Vine Abiders Bear Beautiful Fruit

> *I am the vine; you are the branches. If a man remains in me and I in him, he will bear much fruit; apart from me you can do nothing. If anyone does not remain in me, he is like a branch that is thrown away and withers; such branches are picked up, thrown into the fire and burned. If you remain in me and my words remain in you, ask whatever you wish, and it will be given you. This is to my Father's glory, that you bear much fruit, showing yourselves to be my disciples.* (John 15:5–8)

Your life will not bear the fruit of the Spirit—love, joy, peace, patience, kindness, goodness, longsuffering (see Galatians 5:22–23)—if you don't abide in the vine. Jesus is the true vine, but there are many false vines that tempt us to abide in them. To *abide* is "to remain; continue; stay; to continue in a particular condition, attitude, relationship, etc." When we abide in anything other than the true vine, we will experience stress and turmoil in life's storms, get burned out trying to figure out how to make it through, and attempt to deal with our storms in worldly, carnal ways. But when we remain in the Lord's presence and submit to His Word, we will come through every storm unscathed.

Your source of strength and sustenance is whatever vine you're abiding in. Are you getting your vitality, your confidence, and your emotional nourishment from something other than the true vine? When we abide in anything but the Lord, our chances of survival are severely diminished. When we abide in false vines, they produce false fruit in our lives—a false sense of security, a false sense of peace, a false sense of acceptance, and a false sense of importance. But when we abide in the true vine—Jesus—through prayer, worship, and the study of His Word, we can produce great fruit.

Vine Abiders Welcome the Pruning Process

I am the true vine, and my Father is the gardener. He cuts off every branch in me that bears no fruit, while every branch that does bear fruit he prunes so that it will be even more fruitful.　　　(John 15:1–2)

Our heavenly Father is the gardener, and He prunes us to make us more fruitful. If we desire to bear fruit and be standard setters who radiate God's glory, we must submit to the pruning process. *Prune* means "to cut or lop off superfluous or undesired twigs, branches, or roots from; trim; to rid or clear of (anything superfluous or undesirable)." Father God is the one who does the pruning, so we can stop blaming those around us; it's not them, it's God. Many people don't like to submit to the pruning process, and so they become "prunes" of spiritual dryness, bitterness, and anger, instead of getting pruned. I want to challenge you not to become a "prune" but to submit to the pruning process. Allow the Lord to produce great fruit in you through the difficult times of your life.

Yes, I said through the difficult times. If we'll let Him, God will use the storms of life to prune us so that we can be even more fruitful. Anything Satan means for evil, God will use for good, if we only keep our hearts right. As it says in Romans 8:28, *"We know that all things work together for good to those who love God, to those who are the called according to His purpose."*

We all know what a prune is—it's a dried-up plum. Don't become a dried-up piece of fruit in the kingdom of God! Your heavenly Father wants your life to be fruitful. If we have dried-up, rotten fruit in our lives, we won't be desirable or beautiful to anyone, including the Father. That kind of fruit does not bring Him glory.

The branches that don't produce fruit, the Lord cuts off. But the branches that do produce fruit, the Lord prunes, so they will be even more fruitful. That's what He wants to do in your life and in my life today. Father God wants to prune us so we will be even more fruitful for His kingdom—simply submit to the pruning process. It will be over before you know it!

Keep Abiding in the Vine

There is a crepe myrtle tree in the front of my house. When I first bought my house, it was springtime. The tree had been pruned back to the point that I didn't even recognize what type of tree it was—not that I have any skill in identifying flora and fauna. Anyway, within a month or two, this little tree that had started as just a group of stubs started blooming. Four months later, the tree was huge! After five months, I started thinking I needed to prune the tree because it was growing so fast. It was a gorgeous tree, but its bushiness was beginning to detract from its beauty.

> Anything Satan means for evil, God will use for good, if we only keep our hearts right.

The same is true for you and me. When we abide in the vine, we blossom and begin to produce fruit. And God needs to prune us regularly so that we won't grow wild. You don't want to grow out of control and lose the beauty of your fruitfulness. My crepe myrtle tree would damage my house if I didn't prune it each year. Your ministry, your business, your organization, or whatever you're doing can grow so fast that it becomes overgrown and harmful. It's best to be pruned regularly. That way, the fruit stays beautiful and the plant stays healthy.

Our obedience pleases the Lord and attracts the King of Kings. Boaz was attracted to Ruth because of her character and obedience. The king was attracted to Esther because of her obedience. And the Lord is attracted to our heart of obedience for Him.

Just as Ruth and Esther's beauty attracted others, so can ours. Our beauty comes from the glory of God and His anointing. Being in His presence, being obedient to do His will, and living a godly life causes us to glow with His beauty.

Chapter 10: The Beauty Contest

Points to Ponder

1. We become attractive to the Lord, as well as to other people, when we've spent time in His presence. Are you intentional about "abiding in the Vine" on a daily basis? How can you dwell more fully in the Lord's presence all day long?

2. Have you ever been "pruned" by the Lord? Which branch(es) did He cut back or remove? What was the result?

3. What are some of the "false vines" you may have abided in at one time or another? How can you work toward living only in the true Vine?

Meditate on these Scriptures, speak them aloud, and commit them to memory:

*Blessed are those who have learned to acclaim you, who walk in the light of your **presence**, O LORD.*   (Psalm 89:15)

He who dwells in the shelter of the Most High will rest in the shadow of the Almighty.   (Psalm 91:1)

But the fruit of the Spirit is love, joy, peace, patience, kindness, goodness, faithfulness, gentleness and self-control.   (Galatians 5:22–23)

Draw near to God and He will draw near to you.   (James 4:8 NKJV)

PART THREE

TAKE YOUR PLACE IN THE PALACE

— 11 —

STAY COMMITTED

Congratulations! You have completed the preparation process, and now you're in the palace. But the test doesn't stop there! In fact, the true test is only beginning. Making it to the palace is one thing; staying there is something else altogether. The key is to stay committed to the purpose you set out to pursue in the first place. You can't afford to lose sight of your mission or to become lax about the character qualities you just worked so hard to develop.

Queen Esther was a woman of commitment. She was committed to living a life of righteousness. She was committed to fulfilling her call, no matter the cost. So strong was her commitment, in fact, that she was not afraid to die for the sake of her people.

In this day and age, people don't like to make commitments—even simple ones. Husbands and wives walk out on their marriages because they don't "feel like" being committed anymore. Churchgoers leave a church because they "can't commit" to persevering through the difficult times. Leaving during difficult times is almost never God's will. As we've said, God often uses difficult times to do a great work in you, if you'll just stick around instead of running away from His pruning process.

Of course, I'm not talking about leaving an abusive situation or other difficult times that the Lord releases you from. But I am talking about you releasing yourself from your commitment because you don't "feel" like keeping your commitment during the difficult days, weeks, months, or years!

At Joy Ministries, we have some wonderful phone counselors who have volunteered faithfully for years. They always show up on time, a sure sign of commitment. We also have some that aren't very committed. When asked if they could do phones on a particular day, they respond, "I'll try. I will have to see how things go." I have learned that anyone who responds this way is not that committed, and that anything short of total commitment guarantees that a volunteer will not come to our phone center at the scheduled time. Something else will inevitably come up to prevent their fulfilling their obligation. Ninety-nine percent of the time, if they don't commit to being there, they never make it.

We have to be firm in our commitments and we have to purpose to be where the Lord wants us to be at the time He wants us to be there. If not, we will just drift through life, being controlled by our circumstances rather than by the Holy Spirit.

Many Are Called; Few Are Committed

The Word tells us that the Lord has called many people, but only a few are chosen to be used by God. (See Matthew 22:14.) The reason that many are called and only a few are chosen is because of a lack of commitment. Esther was chosen because she was committed. She didn't commit one day and then, the next day, decide the price was too high to pay and back out of the arrangement. She was faithful to her commitment to the King and His purpose for her life.

> *The Spirit of the Sovereign Lord is on me, because the Lord has anointed me to preach good news to the poor. He has sent me to bind up the brokenhearted, to proclaim freedom for the captives and release from darkness for the prisoners, to proclaim the year of the Lord's favor and the day of vengeance of our God, to comfort all who mourn, and provide for those who grieve in Zion—to bestow on them a crown of beauty instead of ashes, the oil of gladness instead of mourning, and a garment of praise instead of a spirit of despair. They will be called oaks of righteousness, a planting of the Lord for the display of his splendor.* (Isaiah 61:1–3)

Yes, the Lord has anointed you to share the good news of the gospel. Yes, the Lord wants to send you to bind up the brokenhearted and to minister healing and deliverance to those in need. You are already called and you are already anointed, but now you need to be committed. Your commitment causes you to be fruitful in the lives of others and your commitment keeps you focused on the end product—*"oaks of righteousness, a planting of the Lord for the display of his splendor."* That's right a display of His splendor for His glory, not ours!

Commitment keeps you focused on the fruit for the Father and for His kingdom. Commitment causes you to be fruitful and keeps you focused once you are fruitful. God didn't bring Esther to the palace for her own benefit; God brought Esther to the palace for the people. God didn't bring Joseph to Pharaoh's palace for himself; God brought Joseph to the palace for the people. God always wants to use us and promote us for the sake of His people and His kingdom. As we are committed to the Father's purpose, that commitment causes us to stay focused on the fruit once we cross the finish line and enter the palace.

Esther could have lost sight of why God put her in the palace and she could have used her position for personal gain. Joseph could have used his place of promotion with Pharaoh as a place of revenge against the ones who hurt him the most—his own brothers. But Joseph knew God had brought him there for the sake of the people, including his own family.

> *Then Joseph said to his brothers, "Come close to me." When they had done so, he said, "I am your brother Joseph, the one you sold into Egypt! And now, do not be distressed and do not be angry with yourselves for selling me here, because it was to save lives that God sent me ahead of you. For two years now there has been famine in the land, and for the next five years there will not be plowing and reaping. But God sent me ahead of you to preserve for you a remnant on earth and to save your lives by a great deliverance. So then, it was not you who sent me here, but God. He made me father to Pharaoh, lord of his entire household and ruler of all Egypt."* (Genesis 45:4–8)

Joseph was committed to God's purpose for His life. His commitment took him all the way to the house of Pharaoh, and his commitment to the Father caused him to forgive and forget all the wrong done to him. Joseph's commitment caused him to be in a place to bless the people, and he stayed focused on blessing the people; it remained his commitment.

Commitment kills selfishness. It's so important that selfishness is eliminated through the testing of our commitment before entering the palace because selfishness cannot live in the palace. The palace position is always for the sake of God's people and not for selfish purposes.

Esther Kept Her Commitment at the Palace

It was commitment that took Esther to the palace, but it was a greater level of commitment that was required once she got there. In order for Esther to fulfill her purpose at the palace, she needed to be committed more than ever. She had to be so committed that she was willing to give her life—that's what I call commitment!

Once we conceive a dream or a vision, we must remain committed. Too many people abort the dream or the vision before it's actually birthed. The day I delivered my daughter I had been at the doctor's office that morning. When Dr. Miller examined me, he said, "You are already five centimeters. You are going to have this baby today."

I couldn't say, "Well, I have been thinking about it, and I really don't want to commit to having this baby today. I would rather go shopping and eat chocolate."

Too late—I had already conceived her; I had made the commitment! I was going to deliver that baby, like it or not. Yes, there was some pain, but it was well worth it!

When Esther was about to fulfill her purpose at the palace, her commitment caused her to press past any carnal desire that attempted to derail her from fulfilling the will of the Father.

> *On the third day Esther put on her royal robes and stood in the inner court of the palace, in front of the king's hall. The king was sitting on his royal throne in the hall, facing the entrance. When he saw Queen Esther standing in the court, he was pleased with her and held out to her the gold scepter that was in his hand. So Esther approached and touched the tip of the scepter.*   (Esther 5:1–2)

Esther's commitment caused her to risk her life in an attempt to save the entire Messianic line. Her commitment affected not only her and her people of that day, but her commitment to fulfill her purpose preserved the Messianic line in which Jesus—the Savior of the world—was born. That's huge! I'm sure she had no idea how her commitment would affect the entire world, including you and me today!

Esther's commitment caused her to be willing to lay her life down in going before the king a second time. If Esther had not passed the commitment test the first time, she would have never been chosen for the position as queen. But her commitment needed to be stronger than ever once she took up residence in the palace. So committed was Esther that she was able to say, *"If I perish, I perish."* Wow—that's commitment! The ultimate commitment is proven when someone is willing to lay down his or her life. Esther was more committed than ever. She wasn't just willing to lay down her will, but she was willing to lay down her life!

Our commitment causes us to be chosen for kingdom purposes. Yes, many are called, but few are committed enough to be chosen. I don't know about you, but I want to be committed enough to be among those chosen for kingdom purposes during these last days.

True Commitment Takes Us Out of Our Comfort Zones

Esther completed her God-given assignment in the palace without grumbling and complaining about the price she had to pay. She wasn't focused on her own comforts or agenda; she was committed to God's plan for her life. And so, she succeeded.

Commitment and complacency cannot coexist. When you commit to something, you must be prepared to kiss your comfort zone good-bye. Your comfort zone is what you want to do when you want to do it. Your comfort zone is all about what you want, what you think, and what you feel. But when you are committed, you are willing to get outside of your comfort zone in order to achieve that which you are committed to—your potential zone.

> When you commit to something, you must be prepared to kiss your comfort zone good-bye.

When we have selfish motives, when we are led by selfishness, we can't be committed to anything outside of our comfort zone. But when we are committed, we realize we must press past our comfort zones in order to come into our potential zones. And we must do so without complaining.

True Commitment Doesn't Complain

Standard setters who pass the commitment test do so without complaining. Great leaders are prepared by the Lord to be winners, and winners refuse to be whiners. Whiners never want to get out of their comfort zones. Whiners always talk about how bad they have it and they talk about everything they are going through. Winners, on the other hand, understand that in order to get to

> Winners don't talk about what they are going *through* because they are too busy talking about where they are going *to*.

their potential zone, they will have to get out of their comfort zone. Winners don't talk about what they are going through because they are too busy talking about where they are going *to*. Winners focus on the palace! They don't have time to whine, and they are on the most direct path to the palace.

Whiners are filled with fear; they always think about the "what if's." Fear paralyzes the whiner from stepping out into what God has for him. The winner, on the other hand, takes a bold step of faith and gets out of the boat when the Lord tells him to come.

True Commitment Requires Self-Discipline and Self-Denial

Knowing God's will and His plan for your life isn't a hard thing. But disciplining your flesh and your soul to stay committed to fulfilling God's will for your life is not always easy.

God disciplines us in order to train us. The Word tells us that the Lord disciplines those He loves. (See Hebrews 12:6.) Always welcome the Lord's discipline. Then, make the changes that He shows you to make and "grow forward." I discipline my daughter because I love her and want the best for her. The same is true with the Lord. He disciplines us to bring us into His best for our lives.

God's discipline trains us so we can develop self-control. He wants us to have self-control so that the Holy Spirit can be in control of our lives. He disciplines us so we can have character—the character of Christ. God disciplines us so we can develop orderliness and efficiency in our lives. With orderliness and efficiency in our lives, we can have attainable, God-inspired goals.

Discipline in one specific area of life will help us to be disciplined in every other area. If I stay disciplined to eat healthy and exercise, it's easier for me to stay disciplined to read my Bible and maintain a powerful prayer life daily. But if I slack up in my discipline in eating or exercising, I find it harder to be disciplined in prayer and reading the Word. If I'm disciplined even in my spending, it helps me to be disciplined in other areas of my life.

The Lord wants us to be disciplined enough to make commitments and disciplined enough to keep our commitments. Discipline in other areas of your life helps you to be disciplined enough to keep your commitments. Discipline is contagious.

Esther was given special treatment from the moment she arrived at the palace. She won the favor of everyone, and anything she wanted was given to her. And it was all because of self-discipline. When the other girls were gathering as much jewelry as they could get their hands on, Esther set the standard. Less is often more! The world says different. The world thinks different. The world says, "Get all you can, because more is always better." But that's not true in God's kingdom.

In the kingdom of God, "Less is more" holds true most of the time. The integrity of Esther caused her not to hoard things for herself or for her personal gain. Esther set the standard, but none of the other girls even noticed. They had their own standards, and they could not see past themselves.

Before a girl's turn came to go in to King Xerxes, she had to complete twelve months of beauty treatments prescribed for the women, six months with oil of myrrh and six with perfumes and cosmetics. And this is how she would go to the king: Anything she wanted was given her to take with her from the harem to the king's palace. (Esther 2:12–13)

Now, I can imagine that there was a lot of competition going on. Girls can be a little "catty" anyway. But this was the biggest competition of their lifetime. They were "competing" for the queen's crown.

When I was a teenager, I was in a beauty pageant for my state. It was a real eye-opener for me. Many of the other girls were ruthless and cutthroat. They would do anything to win. I was there with my girlfriend, and we wanted to just have a fun weekend and meet the other girls who had qualified throughout our state. But not everyone felt the same way. And we later discovered that the girl who ended up winning had tried to cheat.

Mine was a small state competition, but Esther was competing for an important role—the next queen for King Xerxes. In spite of everything that was at stake, Esther was not selfishly motivated. Rather, she was committed to fulfilling her God-given purpose.

When the turn came for Esther (the girl Mordecai had adopted, the daughter of his uncle Abihail) to go to the king, she asked for nothing other than what Hegai, the king's eunuch who was in charge of the harem, suggested. And Esther won the favor of everyone who saw her. (Esther 2:15)

Anyone without the character of Esther would have been trying to get everything possible, requesting this and requesting that. She would be grabbing anything and everything she could get her hands on. I'm sure that there were many who were committed to their own selfish gain. They were committed to "pushing" their way to the top. But Esther was committed to the King's purpose. She was submitted and committed. She trusted the wisdom of those in authority over her—in this case, Hegai—and she didn't ask for anything extra. She asked only for what Hegai suggested. That's commitment. Esther had a commitment to excellence, a commitment to godly character, and a commitment to fulfilling her purpose. That's what brought her to the palace.

We must be as Esther, committed to our palace and our purpose in God. None of us will ever get there without getting there on purpose. We have to purposely pursue our purpose in the Lord. It's never going to "just happen." When we are committed, we purposely pursue our purpose in God.

Esther was willing to lay down her life for kingdom purposes. As she prepared to go before the king, not even knowing if she would come out alive, she fasted.

Fasting Requires Commitment

What we do when we are on the brink of a breakthrough says a lot about our relationship with the Lord. When we are in the face of adversity or on the verge of a victory, our preparation for the next step can flow out of the presence of God or out of sin and compromise.

> What we do when we are on the brink of a breakthrough says a lot about our relationship with the Lord.

When Haman, the king's adviser who was plotting against the Jews, found out that he was on the verge of victory, he, along with the king, *"sat down to drink"* (Esther 3:15). His focus shifted from everything around him to himself. He wasn't interested in doing the "dirty work" of delivering the message. When we sit down to drink, when we relax our muscles and focus on our own comfort, we can't walk uprightly with the Lord. We can't walk with integrity, as the Lord desires us to, if we are too busy sitting down. Haman did just that. He focused on himself and how he could indulge his own needs and his own desires.

Esther, on the other hand, fasted. She sent out a proclamation: *"Do not eat or drink for three days, night or day. I and my attendants will fast as you do"* (Esther 4:16). A heart that is focused on the Lord does not concern itself with what is most comfortable or convenient but on giving everything it takes to accomplish the will of God.

Are you committed to living a lifestyle of fasting? When the Lord speaks to us to go on a fast, we often act like He's asking us to give up our lives unto death. Actually, it's a temporary death to our carnal wills and fleshly desires but not a death to our actual body; though we act like we won't make it out alive!

> Fasting doesn't move God, but it does move our flesh out of the way long enough for us to hear from Him.

Esther's commitment level enabled her to do both without even batting an eye. It was an immediate response that said, "Yes, I will do whatever it takes." She laid down her life after fasting for three days and three nights.

Fasting is compelling evidence of commitment. Are you committed to hearing the voice of God enough to fast? Are you committed to the fulfillment of the vision enough to fast for God to open doors and show you which way to go?

Often, the Lord is trying to speak to us, but we can't hear His voice over the constant, screaming demands of our flesh. They are so loud that it's obvious to everyone but us. If you have given your flesh center stage and you are listening to its every desire, chances are, you can't hear the still, small voice of the Holy Spirit.

Fasting doesn't move God, but it does move our flesh out of the way long enough for us to hear from Him. Whatever appetite you feed, whatever desire you give into, becomes the strongest voice in your life. If you feed your flesh by giving into its desires whenever it wants something, your flesh will become the strongest. If you feed your spirit the Word, if you stay in the presence of the Lord you will crave the things of God and your spirit man will become the strongest.

We must make sure that our spirits are stronger than our flesh. As we control our flesh and feed our spirits, we set ourselves up to hear the voice of God. We must also have what I call "soul control." "Soul control" comes when you commit to self-discipline. When you are controlled by your soul, you are constantly giving into what you want, what you think, and what you feel. That's all the soul does all day long—it tells you what you want, what you think, and how you feel. But when your soul and your flesh are submitted under the stronger desires of your spirit, you are led by what the Holy Spirit wants, what God thinks about the situation, and what the will of the Father is in every situation and circumstance.

Fasting helps you get to that place of being "spirit-man dominated." Don't allow anything to dominate you except for the Spirit of the Lord on the inside of you. As you live a lifestyle of fasting and prayer, you can hear the voice of the Lord concerning the direction and the will of the Father. Consider committing to fast whenever the Holy Spirit leads you and commit today to maintain a powerful prayer life. As you maintain a prayer life, you will know when the Holy Spirit wants you to fast. And then, you must follow through with it. Don't ignore the nudging of the Holy Spirit to fast. God is waiting to meet with you during an intimate time of fasting and prayer—don't miss out on what He wants to say to you!

Fasting shows your commitment to die to the flesh for kingdom purposes. Don't fast to lose weight—that's not a commitment to hear the voice of God for kingdom purposes. That's a commitment to maintain your waistline. Yes, you should be committed to having a healthy weight, but using fasting to do so instead of using fasting for spiritual purposes is no more than binging and purging.

What Are You Committed To?

How we spend our money and whatever we spend it on shows a lot about our commitment. I have never been a pet lover, partially due to allergies. My daughter, on the other hand, loves dogs. Actually she loves most animals, but dogs are her favorite, hands down!

To make a long story short, God spoke to me and told me to get her a dog. Believe me, it took a Word from the Lord for me to do that one! Destiny had wanted a dog for as long as she could talk.

There is only one dog breed that I'm not allergic to, and that's the Maltese. So, for Christmas one year, I bought her a little five-pound Maltese. I wanted a small one because small dogs eat small and doo-doo small. (Small doo-doo piles seemed a lot more manageable to me.)

When we got the dog, Destiny named her Miracle because she said it was a miracle that I'd let her get a dog—and it definitely was! Miracle soon adopted the nickname Mi-Mi (for a double Miracle).

Soon after I'd brought Mi-Mi home, something began to happen to me. I fell in love with this dog! I couldn't believe it. I even treated her like my own daughter, buying her gifts whenever I traveled, as I've always done for Destiny. I would find myself flying home from California with a gift I'd bought for Mi-Mi because I'd missed her so much!

I couldn't believe myself. Before Mi-Mi came into my life, whenever I would see a poster that said "Lost Dog," I would think to myself, *Why not just go buy another dog?* I didn't understand that these little furry creatures were members of the family! You don't just go buy another sister or another little brother, but I didn't get it.

I finally got it! I became so committed to this animal that I started spending my hard-earned money to buy this dog bows for her head—and that was just the beginning! Now, I've graduated all the way up to buying a doggie stroller so we can take her to the mall with us. Yes—that's right— she goes to the mall and everywhere else with us. I'm still shocked when I think about it.

But my commitment to loving this little five-pound pooch has caused me to give not only my love and my time, but also my finances. When we are committed to something, we spend our money on it. And wherever we spend our money shows where our hearts are committed, for *"where your treasure is, there your heart will be also"* (Matthew 6:21).

When we are committed to advancing the kingdom of God, we will give generously of our finances in the forms of tithes and offerings. You can say you're committed all you want, but if you are truly committed, your giving will prove it. Have you heard the saying "The proof is in the pudding"? Well, the proof is also in your wallet—the proof of where your heart and your commitment are.

Are you committed enough to the vision and the purpose to open your wallet, to write a check, to be the first to give? If you aren't committed enough to give financially, you really aren't committed enough—I love you enough to tell you the truth.

As standard setters, we need to be committed to the call of God on our lives. We need to be committed to the vision of the ministry that God has given us. We must be committed to our relationships and to our loved ones.

These days, not many people like to make a commitment so they miss out on all the blessings that result from commitment. The ultimate commitment is that of covenant commitment. God is the creator of covenants and when we have covenant commitment, we reap covenant blessing. Marriage of course is a covenant commitment, but we can also have covenant connections and covenant commitments to a ministry, to friends and family, to our place of employment, etc.

Covenant Commitments

A *covenant* is "an agreement, usually formal, between two or more persons to do or not do something specified." In a covenant relationship, we don't think about ourselves but rather prioritize the well-being of the other person. When we have a covenant relationship with another person, it actually means we are willing to have him benefit at our own expense.

If all of the people who got married would commit to their spouses' benefit at their own expense for the rest of their lives, we wouldn't have such a high divorce rate. Even though that's what their covenant vows actually mean, most newlyweds go into the marriage covenant thinking about how they are going to benefit personally. That's a recipe for disaster. But God loves us so much that He works that self-centeredness out of us if we allow Him to.

God is a God of covenant. He wants us to be covenant people who remain committed to serving Him, to serving other people, and to fulfilling His purpose for our lives.

> *He remembers his covenant forever, the word he commanded, for a thousand generations, the covenant he made with Abraham, the oath he swore to Isaac. He confirmed it to Jacob as a decree, to Israel as an everlasting covenant: To you I will give the land of Canaan as the portion you will inherit.* (Psalm 105:8–11)

Father God never forgets His covenant with us. Maybe others have forgotten or have chosen to forget their covenants with you, but the Lord never forgets His covenant! It's everlasting, through thick and thin, through the good times and through the hard times. The Lord's covenant commitment to you will endure forever, and yours should, as well, if you expect to endure in the palace.

Chapter 11: Stay Committed

Points to Ponder

1. Have you ever been drawn outside your comfort zone because of your commitment to a God-given vision or cause? What did you do to reinforce your commitment?

2. Commitment to prayer and fasting is an important part of spiritual discipline. Have you incorporated these practices into your life? If not, pray that the Lord would give you guidance as to when and why to fast.

3. Do you have any relationships that could be considered covenant commitments? Assess how much you prioritize those commitments and whether you see them more as opportunities to bless others or to benefit personally.

Meditate on these Scriptures, speak them aloud, and commit them to memory:

But store up for yourselves treasures in heaven, where moth and rust do not destroy, and where thieves do not break in and steal. For where your treasure is, there your heart will be also.   (Matthew 6:20–21)

For many are invited, but few are chosen.   (Matthew 22:14)

The Lord disciplines those he loves, and he punishes everyone he accepts as a son.   (Hebrews 12:6)

— 12 —

Stand on the Truth

Truth should be the very basis of every standard we have. Therefore, if we are to be standard setters, we must proclaim the truth not only with our lips, but also with our very lives—by our attitudes, actions, and interactions. Esther was not afraid to proclaim the truth boldly, even at the risk of her own life. And we must be the same if we expect to set the standard for this generation.

We have this challenge in Joshua 24:15:

But if serving the LORD seems undesirable to you, then choose for yourselves this day whom you will serve, whether the gods your forefathers served beyond the river, or the gods of the Amorites, in whose land you are living. But as for me and my household, we will serve the LORD.

When you decide to serve the Lord, you must be bold about it. The unbelievers in this world are bold about serving their gods. Those who practice other religions are bold about serving their gods. We servants of the one true God must be bolder than ever in serving and proclaiming our God—the King of Kings and Lord of Lords! Make sure that it's obvious whom you serve.

Esther took a big chance when she appeared before the king without having been summoned and pleaded the case of her people.

All the king's officials and the people of the royal provinces know that for any man or woman who approached the king in the inner court without being summoned the king has but one law: that he be put to death. The

only exception to this is for the king to extend the gold scepter to him and
spare his life.   (Esther 4:11)

Esther knew the risks involved. She was acutely aware that her actions could cost her everything. She knew her life was on the line. But she also knew that she had to proclaim the truth if her people were to be saved from perishing.

> *On the third day Esther put on her royal robes and stood in the*
> *inner court of the palace, in front of the king's hall. The king was*
> *sitting on his royal throne in the hall, facing the entrance. When he*
> *saw Queen Esther standing in the court, he was pleased with her*
> *and held out to her the gold scepter that was in his hand. So Esther*
> *approached and touched the tip of the scepter. Then the king asked,*
> *"What is it, Queen Esther? What is your request? Even up to half the*
> *kingdom, it will be given you."*   (Esther 5:1–3)

Esther pressed past her fears and boldly proclaimed the truth, and the result was that an entire nation was saved. We are in a day and an hour in the body of Christ where we *must* boldly proclaim the truth. As we press past our fears—all of our fears—and speak the Word of truth with love and boldness, God will use us to be standard setters in these end times.

The world boldly proclaims its secular values in the face of believers all the time. Followers of false religions boldly proclaim their doctrines all the time. As born-again believers, we must be just as bold—bolder, even—in proclaiming the Word of truth.

> We can't boldly proclaim the truth if we aren't boldly *living* the truth ourselves.

We can't boldly proclaim the truth if we aren't boldly *living* the truth ourselves. If we are living with a mixture of righteousness and unrighteousness, we can be sure that the Holy Spirit will boldly proclaim that fact to us. He may not speak audibly to us, and that is why we must be still before the Lord long enough for Him to correct us and direct us. As we maintain an intimate prayer life with the Lord, we get still before the Lord in His presence on a regular basis. It's during those times that we can hear the still, small voice of the Lord. That voice corrects us, pruning our hearts and our attitudes. We must yield to His discipline before we can qualify to proclaim truth to this generation.

And His discipline always works toward uprooting the mixture from our lives, a charge we are given to perform in the lives of others.

Get the Mixture Out

Around the end of the year 2010, God spoke to me and told me that He wanted the church—the body of Christ—to get mixture out so that the power could get back in. What is "mixture"? Mixture is what occurs when we compromise our standards and tolerate sin in our hearts. If left untreated, mixture tends to infiltrate our homes and churches. We must get all instances of mixture out of our lives if we are to maintain godly character and live by high standards. For it is only when we have eliminated mixture from our hearts and our homes that we can clear away all mixture from the body of Christ—the church.

I believe we are entering a time in the Lord when our choices will make it or break it for us. I believe there will even be times for some people where their very lives will depend upon their choices.

It's so important that we hear from God daily and that we walk in obedience to His voice. A wrong choice or a wrong decision can cause us to lose everything.

Mixture and compromise can cause us to be unable to clearly hear the voice of God. There was mixture in Lot's heart, and the result was that he could not clearly hear from God. And you can't stand on the truth you don't know!

Mixture and Its Consequences in the Life of Lot

Lot looked up and saw that the whole plain of the Jordan was well watered, like the garden of the LORD, like the land of Egypt, toward Zoar. (This was before the LORD destroyed Sodom and Gomorrah.) So Lot chose for himself the whole plain of the Jordan and set out toward the east. The two men parted company. Abram lived in the land of Canaan, while Lot lived among the cities of the plain and pitched his tents near Sodom.   (Genesis 13:10–12)

We know Lot had mixture in his heart because the Word says that he *"chose for himself."* Choosing for yourself is never smart! Lot chose what looked good in the natural but failed to call on God for His opinion in the matter. Mixture in Lot's heart almost cost him his life—as you may know, Sodom and Gomorrah were destroyed by fire because of the Lord's wrath. (See Genesis 19.)

Mixture comes into our hearts when we allow anger, unforgiveness, bitterness, and other sinful attitudes to coexist with kindness, forgiveness, love, and self-control. We can't afford to entertain deadly emotions—that's mixture! We can't allow a little bit of sin and compromise to sneak into our lives—that's mixture. The Word gives us the analogy of little foxes that come to *"ruin the vineyards"* and steal the fruit of our lives. (See Song of Songs 2:15.) When we allow mixture to go on in our hearts, we make way for the "little foxes" and forfeit what could have been an abundant harvest of spiritual fruit.

Lot's uncle Abraham, on the other hand, sought God's will for his every move. Abraham had a pure heart before the Lord—a heart without mixture. Wherever he went, he made an altar to the Lord. He always listened to God's voice and followed obediently.

> *So Abram left, as the LORD had told him; and Lot went with him. Abram was seventy-five years old when he set out from Haran. He took his wife Sarai, his nephew Lot, all the possessions they had accumulated and the people they had acquired in Haran, and they set out for the land of Canaan, and they arrived there.*   (Genesis 12:4–5)

Abraham arrived at his destination because he had sought God every step of the way. He let God do the choosing for him; he didn't choose for himself. When we refuse to permit mixture in our hearts and lives, we, too, will reach our God-ordained destination.

> *The LORD said to Abram after Lot had parted from him, "Lift up your eyes from where you are and look north and south, east and west. All the land that you see I will give to you and your offspring forever."*   (Genesis 13:14–15)

God showed Abraham all that He had for him after he had separated from Lot. Lot represents compromise. Sometimes, it's necessary to cut ties in order to keep the mixture out. If we are still connected with those who are living in mixture, we will have a dim vision, if that, of what God has for us.

God went on to tell Abraham that all that he could see would be his. This illustrates an important concept: God never gives us something that we don't first see. If you can see it in the spirit, it will be manifested in the natural for you.

Mixture opens the door to deception, and the more oblivious you are to the mixture, the more likely you are to be deceived. You don't think there is anything wrong with what you are doing. You are deceived into thinking you are all right. You are deceived into thinking you are hearing from God.

Sometimes, we make decisions based on emotions—fear, anger, lust, and so forth. This is mixture! Our decisions ought to be based on the will of God, but we can hear from Him and discern His will only if we have eliminated mixture from our hearts.

Let's check in with Lot. He pitched his tent near Sodom. (See Genesis 13:12.) Sodom, as you may know, was a wicked city, full of sin and compromise. We must be selective about where we pitch our "tent," which represents where we live or dwell. Lot pitched his tent and took up residence at a place of mixture, but he didn't even realize it. He was deceived.

I can imagine that Lot thought, *I'm not living in Sodom, just on the outskirts.* However, just one chapter later, to the verse, we find out that Lot was no longer living near Sodom. He was living in Sodom. *"They also carried off Abram's nephew Lot and his possessions, since he was living in Sodom"* (Genesis 14:12).

You can never "pitch your tent" near sin and think it won't affect you, for it surely will. If you spend your time near sin, it won't be long before you, too, are living in sin and mixture. When you are exposed to mixture, it's only a matter of time until you're deceived.

Jesus hung around with sinners, but He was the epitome of spiritual perfection and self-denial. He had no mixture whatsoever in His heart. You aren't Jesus! Remember, *"the spirit indeed is willing, but the flesh is weak"* (Matthew 26:41 NKJV; Mark 14:28 NKJV). When you're seeking out someone to convict of sinful behavior, don't make it an "undercover mission" or go as an embedded agent. You can't afford to come under the influence of mixture.

Don't Live in Mixture; Expose It

King Xerxes was not aware of his adviser Haman's plot to annihilate the Jews. He had no clue that there was mixture in the palace. In the biblical record, Esther, who represents righteousness, rose to power just a few verses before the promotion of Haman, who represents mixture. Although mixture existed within the kingdom, even in its leadership, Esther managed to root it out by revealing it for what it was. She was called *"for such a time as this"* to expose mixture in the kingdom and be a voice of righteousness.

The same is true of you today. You are called "for such a time as this" to be a voice of righteousness for the kingdom of God and to expose mixture for what it is. Jesus said, *"There is nothing concealed that will not be disclosed, or hidden that will not be made known"* (Matthew 10:26). God is exposing mixture today, just as He did in the day of Esther, and He needs standard setters to be a voice proclaiming truth as Esther did.

As you live a life of holiness and righteousness, people who live in mixture (sin and compromise) become convicted when you are around them.

I can usually tell when a close friend or family member is not living right because that person tends to avoid me. She will go out of her way not to be around me. When people aren't living right and know it deep down, they may attack you and say, "Are you judging me?" Meanwhile, they are being convicted by the presence of God in your life. I have also known born-again believers living in sin who, when confronted about the mixture in their lives, would say, "That's not holiness; that's bondage. Don't condemn me."

A holy, righteous life is not a life lived in bondage. On the contrary, it's the essence of freedom! True freedom is available only to those who live holy lives. It's living in sin that constitutes bondage.

Ephesians 5:11–14 exhorts us,

Have nothing to do with the fruitless deeds of darkness, but rather expose them. For it is shameful even to mention what the disobedient do in secret. But everything exposed by the light becomes visible, for it is light that makes everything visible. This is why it is said: "Wake up O sleeper, rise from the dead, and Christ will shine on you."

> In many cases, it isn't necessary to say even one word, for the presence of the Lord in your life will do all the talking.

God wants your lifestyle to expose the evil deeds of darkness. In many cases, it isn't necessary to say even one word, for the presence of the Lord in your life will do all the talking. Whether or not you use words, there are some keys that are crucial to follow as you stand on the truth.

Be Bold and Confident in Christ

The writer of Hebrews exhorts us, *"Do not throw away your confidence; it will be richly rewarded. You need to persevere so that when you have done the will of God, you will receive what he has promised"* (Hebrews 10:35–36).

Confidence and boldness are closely connected. If the enemy can steal your confidence, he can steal your boldness. Freedom breeds boldness—Holy Spirit boldness. True freedom is found only in a relationship with Christ. Confidence breeds boldness. The fruit of having hope is a life filled with boldness and freedom.

We need to be confident about who we are in the Lord, and we need to be confident in the Lord's ability through us, in order to pursue the promises of God for our lives. Esther was placed in the palace for a purpose. You, too, have a palace purpose. But unless you are bold and confident in Christ, you will have a difficult time fulfilling your palace purpose.

You can be confident when you know who you are in Christ. Confidence is required for you to walk in Holy Ghost boldness. Boldness is required for you to walk in faith at the level in which Father has called you to operate.

The devil tries to steal your confidence through his lies, which contradict the Word of God. This attempt to steal your confidence through lies usually starts in childhood. The enemy tries to steal your confidence by coming immediately to steal the Word of God. (See Mark 4:15.) The Word of God is the truth that sets you free from every lie. That's exactly why the enemy comes immediately to steal the Word from you.

Your confidence can be stolen by having compromise or mixture in your life. When you are not living right with the Lord, the enemy tries to steal your confidence that the Lord loves you. He tries to get you to back down and not pray. When you have opened the door to sin in your life, you need to boldly come before the throne of grace and ask forgiveness. Then go forward with boldness and confidence that the Lord loves you.

The Lord tells us in the Word that He will never leave us nor forsake us. *"When you lie down, you will not be afraid; when you lie down, your sleep will be sweet. Have no fear of sudden disaster or of the ruin that overtakes the wicked, for the LORD will be your confidence"* (Proverbs 3:24–26). Those verses alone are enough to give us confidence!

Allow the Lord to be your confidence today. As you are confident in the Lord, you can boldly proclaim the truth as a standard setter. All palace personnel must be bold and confident in Christ more than ever before. We don't have to fear anything. We don't have to fear new responsibilities, we don't have to fear concerning our safety or the safety of our loved ones, and we don't have to fear about God's provision for us.

Speak with Holy Spirit Boldness

Jesus said, *"But you will receive power when the Holy Spirit comes on you; and you will be my witnesses…to the ends of the earth"* (Acts 1:8). The Holy Spirit is power from God for us to boldly proclaim the truth! We can use our power for the glory of God or we can sit on our power.

Esther was filled with Holy Spirit boldness, which Jesus guaranteed to give His disciples when He ascended into heaven. He said, *"I am going to send you what my Father has promised; but stay in the city until you have been clothed with power from on high"* (Luke 24:49). They were told to *"stay."* Sometimes, we don't stay in the presence of the Lord long enough to get all that the Father has for us, including Holy Spirit boldness. Sometimes, we don't stay long enough to hear what the Lord wants to say to us. We stay long enough in the presence of the Lord to get all of our requests off our chests, but we don't stay long enough to listen to the voice of the Holy Spirit.

What are you doing with your power? We must use the power we have received from on high to be witnesses for the Lord if we want to be standard setters.

There are times when we need to love someone enough to tell them the truth. And that's what Samuel did. He told Saul the truth about his sinful behavior.

> *"Stop!" Samuel said to Saul. "Let me tell you what the LORD said to me last night." "Tell me," Saul replied. Samuel said, "Although you were once small in your own eyes, did you not become the head of the tribes of Israel? The LORD anointed you king over Israel. And he sent you on a mission, saying, 'Go and completely destroy those wicked people, the Amalekites; make war on them until you have wiped them out.' Why did you not obey the LORD? Why did you pounce on the plunder and do evil in the eyes of the LORD?"*   (1 Samuel 15:16–19)

Saul was trying to convince himself and everyone else that he had followed the Lord's instruction, when indeed he had not. Saul bowed down to compromise because he feared the people more than he feared God.

It can be nerve-wracking to convict those we love and hold them accountable. If you worry about knowing the "right thing" to say, relax, because God will give you the words, just as He did for Moses when He gave him the charge to speak the truth to the Egyptian pharaoh and demand that he release the Israelites from bondage.

> *Moses said to the* LORD, *"O Lord, I have never been eloquent, neither in the past nor since you have spoken to your servant. I am slow of speech and tongue." The* LORD *said to him, "Who gave man his mouth? Who makes him deaf or mute? Who gives him sight or makes him blind? Is it not I, the* LORD*? Now go; I will help you speak and will teach you what to say."*

Conquer Your Fear

If you are filled with fear—fear of any kind—you may have a hard time boldly proclaiming the truth. God wants to reveal any fear or any root of fear that may be in your life. Fear can cripple you and prevent you from fulfilling the will of God in your life.

Fear and depression are closely connected. If a spirit of fear is allowed to take root in your life, it can grow into depression. It's important that we allow the Holy Spirit to reveal any roots of fear and then we must allow the Holy Spirit to set us free in that area.

You may fear abandonment, rejection, or being alone. You may fear failure or you may even fear success. You may fear that you won't be provided for or you may fear any number of other things that the enemy has tried to plague you with. Maybe you fear people or speaking in front of people.

Allow the Holy Spirit to set you free today. God hasn't given you a spirit of fear but God has given you a spirit of power and love, along with a sound mind. (See 2 Timothy 1:7.) If God hasn't given you a spirit of fear, then where do you think it came from? It came right from the pit of hell, and you need to send it back there!

Exercise the authority that the Lord has given you in the name of Jesus and stand your ground! God has given you a sound mind, so why are you allowing the devil to mess with you? You have the mind of Christ, so stand on what you know to be truth and don't allow any fears to have a place in your life.

Standard setters always boldly proclaim the truth, no matter the situation or circumstance. Paul is a good example. Even when the poor guy was being hauled off to prison, he kept proclaiming the truth with boldness. His opponents threatened to kill him, but he kept proclaiming the truth.

Paul was following the example of Jesus. His detractors tried to throw Him over a cliff (see Luke 4:28–30), but He boldly continued about His Father's business.

When we are boldly proclaiming the truth, we walk right through the crowd of opposition, and we boldly get on our way. A little opposition didn't stop Esther. A little opposition didn't stop Paul. A little opposition didn't stop Jesus. And a little opposition shouldn't stop you!

Stand on the Truth, No Matter the Cost

Esther 4:14 says, *"For if you remain silent at this time, relief and deliverance for the Jews will arise from another place, but you and your father's family will perish. And who knows but that you have come to royal position for such a time as this?"*

Esther had to be focused more than ever when faced with the challenge to speak up and boldly proclaim the truth. The king is calling you and bringing you to a royal position for such a time as this in our nation and in the world. God raised up Esther for the very time that she lived in, and God has raised you up for such a time as the one we are living in today. Will you speak the truth in love?

Chapter 12: Stand on the Truth

Points to Ponder

1. How bold are you about proclaiming the truth to fellow believers? To unbelievers?

2. In order to be effective in speaking the truth to others, it's crucial to consider your audience, for the same argument that will convict a fellow believer may fall on deaf ears of an unbeliever. How can you craft your message to reach your intended audience without watering it down?

3. Describe "mixture" in your own words. What are some examples of mixture you've noticed in your particular corner of the world? In your own life?

Meditate on these Scriptures, speak them aloud, and commit them to memory:

*L*ORD*, who may dwell in your sanctuary? Who may live on your holy hill? He whose walk is blameless and who does what is righteous, who speaks the truth from his heart.*   (Psalm 15:1–2)

*Have no fear of sudden disaster or of the ruin that overtakes the wicked, for the L*ORD *will be your confidence and will keep your foot from being snared.*   (Proverbs 3:25–26)

As iron sharpens iron, so one man sharpens another.   (Proverbs 27:17)

There is nothing concealed that will not be disclosed, or hidden that will not be made known.   (Matthew 10:26)

Have nothing to do with the fruitless deeds of darkness, but rather expose them.   (Ephesians 5:11)

— 13 —

SET A STANDARD IN YOUR "PALACE"

The Lord has called us all to be standard setters in every area of life, and it starts where we spend the majority of our time—in the home. What better place to practice modeling high standards? As parents, we must set high standards for our children, and we do this more by how we live than what we say to instruct them. You may tell them, "Do as I say, not as I do," but that never works. Our actions always speak louder than our words, especially to our children, who don't miss much and usually aspire to be just like us.

As parents, we set the standards and guidelines by which we expect our children to live. As we demand that they uphold certain standards, we are used as instruments of God to cultivate Christlike character in our children. In that sense, standards and character development starts in the home, a truth expressed by William Ross Wallace in his poem "The Hand That Rocks the Cradle Is the Hand That Rules the World."

The Seed and the Soil

For years, I had a yard of picture-perfect green grass. Then, all of a sudden, dark brown patches started appearing all over the place. They started out small, but, within a month, they covered a significant part of the yard. I contracted a different landscaping company to take care of the problem, and I asked them to reseed the yard.

When the workers showed up to assess the situation, one of them said to me, "Ma'am, you have a soil problem. It's not a seed problem. It's a soil problem." He went on to tell me that if I didn't treat the soil problem, it wouldn't get any better. The grass seed wasn't the problem—the soil was the problem. I could have spread all the seed I wanted and left the sprinkler on all day, but it wouldn't have made a difference.

Similarly, we can shower our kids with all of the love and support we can muster, but if we haven't given them good soil in which to grow—if we haven't modeled godly lifestyles and upheld standards of discipline—we doom them to fail, just like my dead grass. Our homes are the "soil" where our children are "planted" and take root. Let's make sure to provide them with nutrient-rich soil that's full of healthy boundaries and high standards, so that they may be rooted deeply in the Lord and go on to thrive in every sphere of life.

As was the case with my lawn, the seed is never the problem. If our children—our seed—are not thriving, they're not the problem. It's the soil in which they're planted that's the problem! In the years that I've been a pastor, I have seen dozens of parents bring their children in for counseling. They want the pastor to "fix" their child. But what really needs fixing, most of the time, is the soil—the home "turf." It isn't the seed.

Our children are our seed that God has blessed us with; but, as parents, our standards maintain the soil conditions in our homes in which the seed is expected to grow. If there's a problem with the soil, the seed will have problems and struggle to thrive.

Parents, we must be standard setters with our children, first and foremost, and uphold high standards in the home. The higher your standards, the better the soil. The better the soil, the stronger, healthier, and taller your seed is going to grow.

> The higher your standards, the better the soil. The better the soil, the stronger, healthier, and taller your seed is going to grow.

I can't count how many times my daughter has requested to do something that everyone else is doing. (Of course, "everyone else" is never an accurate count. But, for some reason, kids believe in the power of large numbers to persuade their parents.)

Anyway, I always remind her that I'm not "everyone" else's momma, but I'm her momma, and she's not going to do anything that goes against the standards that I have established for our home.

One day, Destiny informed me that she wanted to load some songs onto her iPod. They were secular songs, sung by an artist who was not a Christian. The standard that I have felt the Lord wanted me to require of my daughter is the same standard and conviction that the Lord put on my heart for me many years ago. Now, I'm not saying that my standard needs to be everyone else's standard—that's between them and the Lord. But, I must maintain the standards the Lord has put on my heart for me and my house—that includes me, my daughter, Destiny, and our dog, Miracle! As for me and my house, we listen strictly to Christian music—end of discussion!

So, this particular day, my daughter was adamant about listening to this singer, because, as Destiny said, "She's not singing anything bad." I went on to explain to her that if the singer wasn't singing anything bad and she wasn't singing anything good, then she fell in the category of neutral. Thank goodness we can rely on God to give us wisdom and the words to speak when we're dealing with our children!

The Lord quickly dropped an example of neutral in my spirit, and I went on to explain that a car in neutral never rolls up hill, but a car in neutral always rolls downhill. When I was a kid, we had these old, junky cars. I can remember having to go outside with my brother to jumpstart our car. We would have to roll the car down the hill in neutral, pop the clutch, jumpstart the car, and drive it back up the hill so that Mom could drive us to school in the mornings. Destiny got a kick out of that story, and she got the point.

I told her that this young girl who was singing "neutral" music was most likely going to roll downhill before too long. I explained to her that our standard was different, and I didn't want her to get in a car that was about to roll downhill. It may look like it's in neutral, but neutral is always a temporary place.

Months later, we walked into a convenience store, and Destiny drew my attention to the magazine rack. On one of the covers was a photo of the singer in a provocative pose and wearing suggestive clothes. Destiny said, "Wow, Mom. You were right."

As we set the "soil" conditions for our children, we can set them up to be standard setters in their generation. God is calling all Esthers. Esthers are those who will dare to be a standard setter in the midst of those who boldly flaunt their lack of standards.

Raise Your Children in the Presence of the Lord

First Samuel 2:21 says, *"And the* LORD *was gracious to Hannah; she conceived and gave birth to three sons and two daughters. Meanwhile, the boy Samuel grew up in the presence of the* LORD.*"*

Samuel grew up in the presence of the Lord. Do you know what your children are growing up in the presence of? What about you? What are you growing up spiritually in the presence of? There are things that you may not have any control over, but there are many choices you can make to assure that your children are being raised in the right presence.

Stay On It

Even though there may be things you have no control over, there are many areas in which you can make good choices—not selfish choices—to help you raise godly children in the presence of the Lord. Too many parents these days choose the easy route. They make selfish choices and end up sacrificing their children as a result.

It takes a lot of work to be a great parent! You have to "stay on it," as I say. When you "stay on it," you know what your kids are watching, what they are listening to, who their friends are, and how those friends are being raised. We must not allow our children to hang around a bunch of spiritual junk. We must watch our words, our actions, and the worldly things we're exposed to. And as we do, we are setting standards and laying a firm foundation that will set our children up for success.

Samuel grew up in the presence of the Lord. As our children grow up in the presence of the Lord, they will be surrounded by the right "stuff" and *"grow in stature and in favor with the* LORD *and with men,"* just as Samuel did. (See 1 Samuel 2:26.)

Hanging out in the presence of the Lord causes you to become like Him. The Word tells us that we become like those we are with. (See Proverbs 13:20.) When we hang out with the Lord, we start acting like Him, we start talking like Him, and we start thinking like Him. Then, as a result, we have His favor. Samuel grew up in the presence of the Lord, and he continued to grow in stature and in favor with God and men. That's exactly what the Lord wants for us and for our children.

When was the last time you spent a few hours to "hang out" in the presence of the Lord in worship and praise? What about your children? Do they see you craving the presence of the Lord? Teaching our children by example to love, respect, and crave the presence of the Lord is one of the best things we could ever do for them. And there's no better way to set our children up for success than that! Then they will be like Samuel, with ever-increasing favor from God and man.

You also must remain the most influential person in their lives. That happens only from spending time with them. There have been so many times when I was exhausted from ministering, but the Holy Spirit would nudge me to go spend time with Destiny. We would just do what teenage girls love to do: talk, shop, and giggle while eating at her favorite places, not mine. As we remain the most significant influence in their lives, we have to inconvenience ourselves and get in their "world."

Look to the Lord for Parenting Wisdom

When Destiny was just four years old, the Lord taught me a valuable lesson in parenting. I was going to enroll her in a preschool that was right around the corner from our house. It was run by one of the best churches in our area. It had a great reputation, and it was very convenient, so I made plans—and never consulted the Lord on the matter.

The Lord woke me up in the middle of the night one evening and said, "You can't always do what's convenient. You didn't even pray and ask Me about this. I want her to go to another school." Well, I was shocked! I couldn't believe that God would want me to send my daughter to a preschool that was a twenty-five-minute drive from our home. And I was shocked because He was right—I hadn't prayed about it.

I have learned that parents are rarely supposed to do the "convenient" thing. Being a great parent after God's heart will often inconvenience you. It will take an extreme amount of time and energy, but it will be the best investment you ever make.

Emphasize Submission to Authority

God established authority and authority roles. He uses authority figures to bring us into our full potential. Although some have misused their authority, God's order is one of godly authority figures used to bring blessing and lead an individual into their full potential.

As a person in authority, our job is to bring those under us into their full potential. If as parents, or others in a position of authority, we don't pay the price of correcting, teaching, and mentoring, there is a huge chance that those under us will be lacking in areas needful to become all that the Lord has for them.

The Greatest Gift You Can Give Your Children

You may wish certain things could be different as you are raising your children. It broke my heart to know that my daughter was going to be raised without a dad in the home. But I'm so thankful that she hasn't been raised without a father—her heavenly Father. The Word tells us that the Lord is a Father to the fatherless. You can't ask for a better Daddy! I have always taught Destiny that a father provides, protects, and loves unconditionally; that's just what her Abba Father does for her. The Lord is the provider of all things. He supernaturally protects her, orders her steps, and loves her just the way she is.

The greatest gift you can give your children can't be bought with money, because you can't put a price on the presence of the Lord. Whether a home is "broken" or not, it's the presence of the Lord that determines the spiritual health and stability of the children who grow up there. As we raise our children in love and discipline, and as God indwells our homes, they will grow up to be what He has ordained for them to be. A stable home depends chiefly upon the head of the home providing an emotionally, physically, and spiritually stable place in which their children can grow and develop in the presence of the Lord.

> The greatest gift you can give your children can't be bought with money, because you can't put a price on the presence of the Lord.

Marriage Commitment to the King

Even if you are a single mother, as I am, never forget that you have a husband—the King of Kings! *"For your Maker is your husband—the LORD Almighty is his name—the Holy One of Israel is your Redeemer; he is called the God of all the earth"* (Isaiah 54:5).

My Maker is my husband, and He is a Father to the fatherless. I have been a single mom since my daughter was two weeks old. It hasn't always been easy. As a matter of fact, I don't believe it's ever been easy. But, you don't need easy—you only need possible. And, with the Lord all things are possible!

The Lord has been a husband to me and the best possible Father to Destiny. Someone just asked me the other day, "Are you just done with the man-thing? Is that why you wear a ring on your finger?" I told them it wasn't that I was done with the "man-thing," but I was just fully committed to raising my daughter and fully committed to fulfilling the call of God on my life. And, at this point in my life, the ring symbolizes to me, and to all the men around me, that I'm committed to the King.

I'm committed to being married to the King. Being married to the King comes with requirements. The first requirement is that of commitment. When you are married to the King, you can't do what everyone else is doing. To whom much is given, much is required. (See Luke 12:48.) But to the person of whom much is required, much will also be given. I have been given much. I have been blessed beyond anything that I could have ever thought or imagined!

The longer you are married, the greater the required commitment becomes. When you have been married for twenty years, the honeymoon phase has long since passed. You have to keep your marriage alive and you choose to stay committed. As you maintain your love relationship with your spouse, you can become closer and more intimate as the years go by.

The same is true with the Lord. As we are married to the King, we should be growing more in love and more intimate with Him as the years go by. Yes, we will meet with times of hardship in our marriages in the natural, as well as in our marriage to the Lord, but those seasons are short in the grand scheme of things. Keep your intimate relationship with the Lord alive by spending time with Him every day, and it will enable you to maintain an atmosphere of His presence in your home.

Chapter 13: Set a Standard in Your "Palace"

Points to Ponder

1. What is your "palace," or primary sphere of influence? Is it your home? Your workplace? Your church? To what degree are you setting a godly standard for the other people in your palace?

2. Have you ever been persecuted for godly behavior? How did you respond?

3. Where can you seek encouragement to keep upholding a standard of Christlike character in your "palace"?

4. Are there any areas of life in which you find yourself following the popular trend instead of setting the standard? What does this reflect about your spiritual life?

5. In the "palace" of a home, what are the most important factors in setting godly standards for children?

Meditate on these Scriptures, speak them aloud, and commit them to memory:

Let your light shine before men, that they may see your good deeds and praise your Father in heaven. (Matthew 5:16)

Do everything without complaining or arguing, so that you may become blameless and pure, children of God without fault in a crooked and depraved generation, in which you shine like stars in the universe as you hold out the word of life. (Philippians 2:14–16)

Dear friends, I urge you, as aliens and strangers in the world, to abstain from sinful desires, which war against your soul. Live such good lives among the pagans that, though they accuse you of doing wrong, they may see your good deeds and glorify God on the day he visits us. (1 Peter 2:11–13)

Conclusion:
The World Is Waiting

The world is longing for standard setters. There are plenty of trend-setters—those who determine what's fashionable to wear and decide what's "cool" to do—but trends never endure. A *trend* is "the general course or prevailing tendency; drift; style or vogue." Trends are simply passing styles that are here today, gone tomorrow.

What this world needs are standards that endure because they're built on the only foundation that's true and eternal: the Word of God. The Word of God never changes because God never changes; He is the same today, tomorrow, and forever. (See Hebrews 13:8.) Righteous living, kingdom character, and uncompromising integrity provide a security unlike anything the world can offer. When we develop those traits, we secure our position in the palace of God's favor, both on this earth and in the life to come.

Though it may seem as if society's values have run amok, believe me, there is a desperate need for those who will take a stand for righteousness and change the world through righteous living. God has called you to greatness—yes, you!—just as He called Esther to greatness. And when God's great standard setters rise to take their place, there's a celebration in the kingdom, just as there was in the palace for Esther. When she rose to her position, *"the king gave a great banquet, Esther's banquet, for all his nobles and officials. He proclaimed a holiday throughout the provinces and distributed gifts with royal liberality"* (Esther 2:18).

Before you were ever born, the Lord called you for His purpose. But you have to answer the call. The very first qualification is simply availability. It's easy to say, "Oh Lord, use me." But then, when the King calls at an inconvenient time that interrupts your agenda, what will you do? Will you say yes to the call? Will you go all the way and pay the price? Or, will you pass on your royal position and allow it to be given to another? I pray not!

We have this challenge in Joshua 24:15:

But if serving the LORD seems undesirable to you, then choose for yourselves this day whom you will serve, whether the gods your forefathers served beyond the river, or the gods of the Amorites, in whose land you are living. But as for me and my household, we will serve the LORD.

When you decide to serve the Lord, you must be bold about it. The unbelievers in this world are bold about serving their gods. Those who practice other religions are bold about serving their gods. We servants of the one true God must be bolder than ever in serving and proclaiming our God—the King of Kings and Lord of Lords! Make sure that it's obvious whom you serve.

Blessed is the man who does not walk in the counsel of the wicked or stand in the way of sinners or sit in the seat of mockers. But his delight is in the law of the LORD, and on his law he meditates day and night. He is like a tree planted by streams of water, which yields its fruit in season and whose leaf does not wither. Whatever he does prospers. (Psalm 1:1–3)

As standard setters, we must put on our "full armor of God" daily. We can't put on just some of our armor. No, we must put on all of our armor, and we must do it daily. Some folks try to survive with a once-a-week "suit-up." In other words, they put on their armor for an hour or two on Sunday morning when they go to church. Then, they try to fight the *"good fight of faith"* all week long, but they struggle because they haven't "suited up" for days.

Ephesians 6:10–18 gives us clear instructions on how to succeed at being standard setters on a daily basis. It reads:

Finally, be strong in the Lord and in his mighty power. Put on the full armor of God so that you can take your stand against the devil's schemes. For our struggle is not against flesh and blood, but against the rulers, against the authorities, against the powers of this dark world and against the spiritual forces of evil in the heavenly realms. Therefore put on the full armor of God, so that when the day of evil comes, you may be able to stand your ground, and after you have done everything, to stand. Stand firm then, with the belt of truth buckled around your waist, with the breastplate of righteousness in place, and with your feet fitted with the readiness that comes from the gospel of peace. In addition to all this, take up the shield of faith, with which you can extinguish all the flaming arrows of the evil one. Take the helmet of salvation and the sword of the Spirit, which is the word of God. And pray in the Spirit on all occasions with all kinds of prayers and requests. With this in mind, be alert and always keep on praying for all the saints.

As a standard setter, you must be strong in the Lord. Don't think for one minute that the strength you need in this day and hour can come from anywhere other than 100 percent from the Lord. As you are strong in the Lord and in His mighty power, you can stand—and set a standard—no matter what opposition comes your way. As a standard setter, you will face opposition and even persecution, sometimes even from other believers. If you are going to be a true standard setter, if you are going to stand even in the midst of persecutions and ridicule, you must have on your full armor.

The apostle Paul went on to say that your battle is not against flesh and blood. Your battle is not against your coworkers, your family members, or the person you sit next to every day. Your battle is against the rulers, authorities, and powers of this dark world—*"the spiritual forces of evil in the heavenly realms."* Don't forget it! You will be tempted to "flesh out" and use carnal weapons to fight with, such as anger, frustration, bitterness, and unforgiveness. But that will never work, except to cause you to forfeit your character and integrity and ultimately lose your place as a standard setter. When you start gossiping and talking about those who are persecuting you, you stoop to their level. If you fail to recognize and remember where the true battle really is, you will fall into the "chicken fight." Remember, the battle isn't against flesh and blood, so don't get yourself all worked up. Getting in a "tizzy" over the situation doesn't do you any good. Actually, you begin to lose the spiritual battle when you start "fleshing out."

The Word goes on to say that you will stand firm when you are dressed in your full armor. Don't try to "stand" as a standard setter without standing firm. Trying to fight in the flesh, or in your own strength, causes you to stand, but not firmly. You stand firm when you are standing on and living out the Word. So, stand firm, and don't position yourself on shaky ground or flimsy principles. All standard setters know how to stand firm, and they dress appropriately, in the full armor of God!

The first specific piece of armor Paul refers to in Ephesians 6 is the belt of truth. All of the armor is very important, and all of the parts are necessary, but I don't think it's a coincidence that the belt of truth is the first part of the armor that's mentioned. If you are going to stand firm, you must be standing on the truth, which is God's Word. If you are going to stand firm, you must be living out the truth and never giving place to the spirit of deception in your life. For you to stand firm, you must be a man or a woman of truth!

Standard setters love the truth and embrace it in every area of their lives. Remember, it's crucial that you not be deceived by the devil's lies. Don't believe what he says about you, your situation, or those around you. If you open the door to deception, you will suffer the consequences.

The good news is, you can put on the full armor of God and stand firm with the belt of truth! The belt of truth causes you to admit and seek help for any problem or area of addiction. Sometimes, things "below the belt" are the hardest areas for people to be open and honest about. The enemy will try to cause shame to overshadow your desire to wear the belt of truth. Statistics show that 50 percent of Christian men are addicted to pornography, and that about one in three pastors is, as well. Come on, folks—let's get honest below the belt! There's a problem here, and God wants to set His people free. But if you try to hide it or cover it up, you will never experience freedom and deliverance, nor will you be chosen as a standard setter in God's kingdom. You must know the truth, including the truth about yourself and your own situation, because the truth will set you free. (See John 8:32.)

Along with the belt of truth, every standard setter must wear the breastplate of righteousness. When you live in righteousness, simply doing the right thing, you can stand firm as a standard setter. The breastplate guards the heart, which is key, because *"out of the overflow of the heart the mouth speaks"* (Matthew 12:34). In addition, Proverbs 4 calls the heart the *"wellspring of life"* (verse 4).

If you aren't wearing the breastplate of righteousness, your heart goes unprotected in the spiritual battles of everyday life—not good! But, when you do the righteous thing, day in and day out, you maintain a godly attitude and an upright heart. Standard setters are always careful to maintain a pure heart before the Lord because they know the importance of standing firm with a right heart.

When you submit to the process of becoming a standard setter, your character grows in holiness and righteousness in a way that causes you to be firmly planted. Make it your goal to grow every day in the Word of God and in righteousness. When you have righteousness in your root system, you'll stand when the storms of life blow your way. And, as you stand firm, others will see and desire to do the same. They'll see your standard and be inspired to follow in suit.

There is an urgent need in the kingdom of God for servants who will inconvenience themselves and their personal agenda, surrender their lives to the King, and be willing to lay down their lives for the sake of His call, just as Esther did. Her character paved the way to the palace, and it will do the same for you. God is calling all Esthers, regardless of age, gender, and race. The King of Kings is calling for all standard setters to arise and report to their palace position. Will you put on your armor and answer the call? Don't miss your chance! The world is waiting.

About Joy Ministries

Joy Ministries seeks to preach the gospel and also to "do" the gospel by reaching out to those who are in need. We don't just administer a program or give temporary relief to people. Our goal is to see lives transformed by God's power and to break the cycle of poverty through discipleship, education, and character development. The following are just a few of our programs that God is using to empower lives:

Joy in the Morning Television Ministry

Though Joy Ministries is not an established church, we bring church services into the homes of millions of people every week. Pastor Danette Crawford reaches into the lives of millions of hurting people through her television broadcast, *Joy in the Morning.* She empowers viewers and brings restoration and healing through her fresh, relevant teachings on various topics.

Mother's Day Celebrations

In 2001, God spoke to Pastor Danette Crawford about the importance of honoring mothers who did not have anyone to honor them on their special day. Since then, God has transformed a small celebration of a few hundred into a celebration for thousands. Every year, single moms, military moms whose husbands are deployed, and widows are invited to attend our Mother's Day Celebration, where they are given a special meal, a gift, and words of encouragement. Their children are also invited to attend and are blessed with a meal and special activities just for them. The invitation is extended to women in all living situations, from low-income housing to battered women's shelters to residential living facilities. Many women come together at this event to celebrate their roles as mothers and to be empowered to live bold lives of freedom and joy through Christ.

Neighborhood Celebrations

It is important that we do not just wait for those in need to come to us; rather, we must pursue them. Held in low-income communities, our Neighborhood Celebrations provide a way for us to befriend the people in the community. We offer carnival games and activities for the children and food and beverages for all participants. In addition, we give away clothes and groceries to every family in attendance. The Neighborhood Celebrations are not meant merely to entertain people but rather to give them an opportunity to begin a relationship with Jesus Christ. We then encourage them to get involved in our other outreaches.

Back to Work

How you feel about your appearance can affect your attitude and even your success. The Back to Work program empowers women in low-income situations by supplying them with professional clothing to wear to work or on job interviews. Women are able to select outfits for themselves at no personal cost and are thereby empowered as their confidence is built.

Bread of Life

We deliver freshly baked bread and pastries to homes in our adopted neighborhoods on a weekly basis. As we distribute the bread, we have the opportunity to pray with the residents for healing, deliverance, and salvation. We aren't just bringing freshly baked bread; we are bringing the *"bread of life"* (John 6:35).

Summer Reading Camp

Summer Reading Camp is an outreach offered in low-income neighborhoods that gives children a chance to learn to read or improve their reading skills. Summer Reading Camps use a fun, "song-focused" curriculum that almost makes the children forget that they are learning. After completing the program, many of the children are able to read above their grade levels.

Lighthouse Learning Centers

Lighthouse Learning Centers are facilities where we hold after-school homework assistance programs for at-risk children living in low-income housing areas. We have several Lighthouse Learning Centers throughout our community, all with certified teachers on staff.

First Day Challenge

The first day of school can be challenging, especially for children who cannot afford the necessary school supplies. Every year, Joy Ministries empowers thousands of children to begin school on the right foot by giving them the school supplies that they need in order to succeed. Each child receives a backpack filled with school supplies and words of encouragement through the gospel message to help him or her start the new school year with confidence. In addition, we bless children with special needs with back-to-school clothes.

Thanksgiving Meals

During this holiday, we reach out to families in need and distribute turkeys, complete with all the trimmings necessary for a Thanksgiving feast.

Holiday of Hope

Every year we extend a dinner invitation to those in need to celebrate the Christmas holiday with us. We use this opportunity to share more than just a meal. We share the hope that is found in Jesus Christ and explain that He wants to give them the gift of life. This celebration brings encouragement to families who otherwise might have spent the holidays discouraged and without a nice meal.

Santa Sacks

Because of financial difficulty, parents are sometimes unable to give gifts to their children on Christmas. Just as God gave the greatest gift of all through His Son, Joy Ministries uses the season of giving to bless families with Christmas gifts and to tell them about the ultimate gift, which is found through the cross. We make dreams become realities as we deliver presents in brightly wrapped paper to the doors of needy families.

Kids Club

At Joy Ministries, we desire that the children affected by our outreaches become men and women of character who will change the world. We hold daily Kids Club outreaches in various low-income, at-risk neighborhoods. The main goals of Kids Club are to see children develop personal relationships with Jesus Christ and to help them develop strong character. Every week, the participants learn about a character trait that they are encouraged to live out. Biblical principles and character traits are emphasized through Bible lessons, songs, games, and crafts. Every child is given a hug and a snack at the end of each meeting. The overall goal is to empower the children by showing them the love of Christ.

The Destiny Scholarship Fund

This particular outreach was established in honor of Pastor Danette Crawford's daughter, Destiny. As a single mom, Pastor Danette looked for assistance in paying for a quality Christian education for her child but found none. Then the Lord spoke to her heart and encouraged her to take a step of faith to be a blessing to others. As a result, the Destiny Scholarship Fund was established. Knowing that each child has a "destiny" for the Lord, she wanted to give children the opportunity to achieve academic excellence in a Christian environment. In addition, as the children from Joy Ministries' adopted neighborhoods grow older, they are able to receive assistance with college expenses through this fund.

Cars for Kids

When cars are donated to us, we don't sell them; we give them to families in need! We bless single-parent or low income families with good, running vehicles that will provide safe transportation to work or school.

Single Moms' LIFE Outreach

It is very difficult to be a single mom, especially when you do not have a good support system. Our Single Moms' LIFE group meets in our outreach center on Friday evenings, and anyone can attend. Single moms receive teaching on how to live victorious, successful lives in Christ. Teaching topics include dealing with loneliness, managing finances, and raising and disciplining children. There are also opportunities to develop new friendships. We also have weekly LIFE groups in our adopted neighborhoods. In addition, the Single Moms' LIFE group outreach assists single parents with paying for rent, food, and utilities; securing jobs; getting their driver's licenses; obtaining and maintaining vehicles; and meeting many other life challenges. Financial counseling is also available through this outreach.

Breakthrough Miracle Services

In the local Hampton Roads area of Virginia, we hold a miracle service on the first Saturday of each month with a great demonstration of the Spirit's power for healing, deliverance, and the prophetic word. Pastor Danette Crawford's messages of hope and encouragement inspire many to press on to a higher level in God.

God Squad

The God Squad is an evangelistic outreach team that goes out into the highways and byways with the gospel message of hope and salvation. We minister in local neighborhoods, at community events, and at various outreaches.

Guy Time/Girl Time Outreaches

The pressures placed upon teenagers are continually growing. Young people are often bombarded with issues at school, in their friendships, and at home. Joy Ministries' Guy Time and Girl Time outreaches offer a safe place for teenagers to share the difficulties that they face in life while simultaneously being discipled into young men and women who have good character and are called to be world changers. Guy Time and Girl Time meetings help teenagers come to a deeper understanding of their identities in Christ and of how that translates into every area of their lives. This outreach also aims to break the cycle of poverty and to reduce crime and teenage pregnancies. We combine teaching with fun activities, along with an annual weekend retreat and other outings.

Empowering Women for Leadership Conferences

These weekend-long encounters with God transform the lives of women from all backgrounds, empowering them to become all that He has called them to be. Through the help of our partners, we are also able to sponsor a number of women who otherwise would not be able to attend.

Fresh Fire Weekends

These weekends, which are held in different cities nationwide, enable people to experience the "fire of God." Under open heavens and without the restraints of time, participants are able to seek God's presence passionately in praise and worship. Encounters with the Holy Spirit are life changing for those in attendance. As Pastor Danette Crawford ministers the Word under a strong prophetic anointing, wounded hearts are mended, strongholds are broken, and individuals are set free by the Word of Truth.

International Miracle Crusades and Conferences

With a desire to reach the hurting and the lost, Pastor Danette Crawford spreads the fire of God in Latin American countries. At each crusade, hundreds of people receive salvation, deliverance, and miraculous healings. City-wide youth crusades are bringing thousands into the kingdom of God, and hundreds of young people are being raised up as evangelists to their countries.

Visit us online at www.joyministriesonline.org.

Prayer Line: 757.420.2625